CONTENTS

1.	When the Righteous Suffer	5
2.	Job's Lament	13
3.	Easy Answers to Hard Questions	21
4.	When Friends Wound	29
5.	The Limits of Human Wisdom	37
6.	Wisdom's Voice	45
7.	The Man I Used to Be	53
8.	The Voice of the Younger Man	61
9.	God Speaks	69
10.	God Speaks Again	77
11.	Job's Repentance	85
12.	Job's Restoration	93
13.	The Message of Job	101

JOB
FROM START2FINISH

MICHAEL WHITWORTH

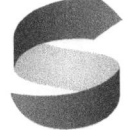

© 2025 by Start2Finish

All rights reserved. No part of this publication may be reproduced, stored in a retrieval system, or transmitted in any form or by any means without the prior written permission of the author. The only exception is brief quotations in printed reviews.

ISBN 978-1-944704-13-1

Published by Start2Finish
Bend, Oregon 97702
start2finish.org

Printed in the United States of America

Unless otherwise noted, all Scripture quotations are from The Holy Bible, English Standard Version®, copyright © 2001 by Crossway Bibles, a publishing ministry of Good News Publishers. Used by permission. All rights reserved.

Cover Design: Evangela Creative

1

WHEN THE RIGHTEOUS SUFFER
JOB 1-2

Objective: To understand that righteous believers may suffer deeply while still trusting in God's sovereign goodness.

INTRODUCTION

In 2006, Amish families in Nickel Mines, Pennsylvania faced a tragedy that shocked the nation. A gunman entered the West Nickel Mines School and killed five young girls. The grief was unimaginable—parents burying children, a tight-knit community shaken to its core. Yet within hours, members of the Amish community publicly expressed forgiveness toward the shooter's family. One father, whose daughter had been killed, told reporters, "We must not think evil of this man." Another explained, "Forgiveness is not something we feel; it is something we practice because God has forgiven us."

Their pain was real, their questions unanswered, but their faith remained steady. They did not claim to understand why such suffering happened. They simply trusted God's sovereignty even when their hearts were breaking. Their response didn't arise from platitudes—it rose from deep, disciplined reverence for God.

Job's story begins in similar terrain. He was upright, faithful, and devoted to God—yet his life unraveled in a single devastating sequence.

Disaster, grief, and physical torment descended without warning. Like the Amish parents, Job faced suffering that defied explanation.

Job 1–2 teaches Christians that faith is not the absence of grief but the decision to trust God in the midst of it. When life collapses, the righteous cling to the One whose goodness does not change.

EXAMINATION

The man from Uz (1:1–5)

Job enters the biblical story not through genealogy or geography but through character. He was "blameless and upright," a man who feared God and turned away from evil. The Hebrew terms describe moral integrity, not sinlessness. Job lived with wholeness before God and consistency before people. His righteousness was real, observable, and sincere—faith that shaped his home, work, and worship.

The text emphasizes his devotion as a father. After his children's feasts, Job rose early to offer sacrifices "just in case" they had sinned in their hearts. That detail reveals a man who believed holiness mattered even in unseen places. His fear of God was neither superstition nor performance; it was reverence woven into the rhythms of daily life.

Nothing in chapter 1 hints at hidden sin or hypocrisy. If anything, Job is presented as the kind of believer people admire—godly, generous, prayerful, prudent, a man whose life shows the beauty of wholehearted obedience. The story begins by establishing Job's righteousness so clearly that when suffering strikes, no one can explain it away as punishment. Job's life challenges the assumption that the faithful should expect immunity from pain.

The heavenly council (1:6–12)

The narrative suddenly shifts to a scene "in the heavenly court," where the "sons of God" present themselves before the Lord. The setting is literary, not a blueprint for angelic meetings, and its purpose is to reveal a truth hidden from human eyes: Job's suffering did not begin on earth. It began in a conversation about the integrity of faith.

Among those present is the satan—literally "the accuser." He is not yet portrayed as the fully developed adversary of later Scripture but as a prosecuting figure who questions human righteousness. God points to Job with delight: "Have you considered my servant Job?" The description echoes the introduction—blameless, upright, God-fearing, and evil-resisting.

The accuser challenges not Job's morality but Job's motives: "Does Job fear God for nothing?" In other words: He serves you because you protect him. Remove the blessings, and his piety will crumble. The satan proposes that Job's faith is transactional—obedience in exchange for prosperity.

This question drives the entire book. Will a believer serve God when the blessings are stripped away? Can humans love God for who he is rather than what he gives? The challenge is not about Job's moral failure but about the nature of genuine faith.

God does not cause evil, but he permits a test that exposes the depth of Job's devotion. Job is placed in the furnace, not because he is unfaithful, but because he is faithful. In the wisdom of God, suffering becomes the stage on which the truth of righteousness is revealed.

A cascade of suffering (1:13–19)

In four rapid calamities, Job's world collapses. Raiders steal his oxen and donkeys; fire consumes his sheep; Chaldeans seize his camels; a desert wind kills his children. The repetition of "while he was yet speaking" heightens the shock. Job is not simply afflicted—he is overwhelmed.

The scale of his loss is staggering. His wealth evaporates, his household crumbles, and the children he prayed for are taken. The narrator gives no hint of moral cause and no explanation. Suffering often arrives unannounced, unearned, and unexplained. The righteous sometimes endure what seems unrighteous.

Job's response is stunning. He grieves—tearing his robe and shaving his head—but he also worships. "The Lord gave, and the Lord has taken away; blessed be the name of the Lord." This is not stoicism but surrendered faith. Job acknowledges God's sovereignty in both blessing and loss. His grief is real, but his trust is deeper.

The narrator affirms: "In all this Job did not sin or charge God with wrong." Faith has been wounded, but not destroyed. Job's devotion survives the first blow.

A second challenge (2:1–6)

The scene returns to the heavenly court. God again points to Job as a model of integrity: "He still holds fast his integrity, although you incited me against him to destroy him without reason." The phrase "without reason" reinforces the theological truth—Job's suffering is not punishment.

The accuser presses further: "Skin for skin!" He claims that Job withstood the first trial because his body was untouched. But if his health collapses, the accuser predicts, Job will curse God. The challenge intensifies: Is Job's faith still genuine when his own flesh is afflicted?

God grants permission with limits: Job may be harmed, but not killed. Divine sovereignty remains intact. The accuser can act only within the boundaries God sets.

Suffering in the body (2:7–10)

Job is struck with "loathsome sores from the sole of his foot to the crown of his head." The imagery suggests chronic, disfiguring pain. Job sits among ashes, scraping his skin with a broken piece of pottery—symbolizing humiliation and helplessness.

His wife, devastated and disoriented by grief, voices the temptation Job has resisted: "Do you still hold fast your integrity? Curse God and die." Her words express not cynicism but despair. She cannot bear the sight of a righteous man destroyed. Yet her counsel echoes the accuser's prediction.

Job responds gently but firmly: "Shall we receive good from God, and shall we not receive evil?" He does not blame God but acknowledges that faith must persist in both prosperity and adversity. The narrator again affirms: "In all this Job did not sin with his lips."

Job's faith has now endured both external loss and internal suffering. Integrity holds, but the internal struggle is just beginning.

The arrival of the friends (2:11–13)

Three friends—Eliphaz, Bildad, and Zophar—come to comfort Job. They are not villains but companions who care deeply for him. When they see Job, they weep, tear their robes, and sit with him seven days without speaking. In their silence, they offer the best comfort they will ever give.

Their presence shows that communal compassion is essential in suffering. Yet the long silence also prepares readers for the painful truth: when the friends finally speak, their words will wound rather than heal. They will assign blame where God has assigned none.

Still, the text gives them dignity in this moment. They mourn with Job before they misjudge him. Their compassion reminds believers that friendship in grief requires humility, not explanations.

Theological foundations in Job 1–2

Job 1–2 lays the groundwork for the entire book:

1. Suffering is not always punishment. Job is righteous, not rebellious. His trials are not the result of hidden sin. Christians must reject simplistic equations between suffering and guilt.

2. God is sovereign even when unseen. The heavenly scenes reveal hidden dimensions of suffering. Believers do not know all the factors, but God does.

3. Faith is tested by trouble, not by theory. The accuser challenges the authenticity of devotion. Job's suffering becomes a testimony that believers can love God without reward.

4. Suffering reveals the depth of righteousness. Job worshiped in grief and remained faithful in pain. His story shows that integrity is proven in adversity, not prosperity.

5. The book of Job is about divine wisdom, not divine cruelty. God does not explain suffering; he transforms the sufferer. The wisdom of God surpasses human attempts to make sense of pain.

6. Renewal begins with honest lament (which will come in chapter 3). Job's silence in chapter 2 prepares for his cry in chapter 3. Suffering pushes believers toward God, not away from him.

APPLICATION

1. Faithfulness is measured in storms, not sunshine

Job's suffering dismantles the assumption that righteousness guarantees an easy life. He served God faithfully, yet his world collapsed without warning. This teaches believers that genuine faith is revealed not when blessings abound but when blessings vanish. Many people follow God for what he gives; Job followed God for who he is. When trials struck, Job grieved deeply, but he did not abandon his devotion. His example challenges Christians to examine their own hearts. Do we serve God only when life is pleasant?

Or do we trust him when prayers go unanswered and circumstances turn dark? Faith grounded in convenience crumbles in crisis, but faith grounded in God's character endures. Job proves that believers can worship even with tears on their faces, because faith anchors itself in the unchanging goodness of God.

2. Suffering does not mean God is displeased

Job 1–2 makes it unmistakable: suffering is not always a sign of divine punishment. Job was righteous, yet he suffered terribly. The friends will later insist otherwise, but the narrator has already declared the truth. This matters for Christians navigating hardship today. Pain does not automatically mean we have sinned or that God has abandoned us. Sometimes righteous people walk through valleys simply because they live in a broken world, or because God is shaping them in ways unseen. When believers assume suffering equals guilt, they burden themselves with false shame and misjudge others. Job's story frees us from that fear. God remained with him even when circumstances suggested the opposite. The cross of Christ confirms the same truth: the most righteous man who ever lived suffered most deeply, proving suffering can coexist with divine favor.

3. Worship is possible even in grief

Job's response to catastrophe is one of the most extraordinary moments in Scripture. He tore his robe, shaved his head, fell to the ground—and worshiped. His grief was raw and honest, yet it did not eclipse his reverence for God. This shows that sorrow and faith are not opposites; they can live in the same heart. Christians do not need to pretend that suffering is small or painless. Like Job, we can lament deeply while still trusting God's sovereignty. Worship in grief is not denial; it is declaration—an affirmation that God is still worthy even when life wounds us. When Christians choose to worship through tears, their faith becomes a testimony to others. Grief becomes an altar on which trust is offered to the God who remains faithful.

4. Integrity must be guarded when suffering tempts the heart

The accuser believed Job would curse God when pain touched his flesh. Job's wife echoed that temptation, urging him to give up. Pain invites shortcuts—bitterness, blame, cynicism, or despair. Yet Job "held fast his integrity." This teaches believers that suffering is not only a physical or emotional trial but a spiritual one. Hardship tests our loyalties. Will we cling to righteousness when obedience costs us? Will we remain faithful when faith seems unrewarded? Integrity is not maintained by willpower alone but by humble dependence on God. The church needs this reminder: trials do not make character; they reveal it. Job's perseverance shows that believers can resist the pull toward compromise by remembering who God is and trusting his wisdom. Suffering may shake us, but it cannot sever our commitment when integrity is anchored in reverence.

CONCLUSION

Job 1–2 pulls back the curtain on a truth every believer must face: faithfulness does not guarantee a painless life. Job loved God earnestly, yet loss and sorrow swept over him without warning. His grief was honest, but his trust endured. He refused to surrender his integrity or abandon reverence. These opening chapters remind Christians that suffering is not always punishment, and God's silence is never absence. Faith holds firm not because life is predictable, but because God is worthy. As the story of Job unfolds, the question is not why the righteous suffer, but how faith survives when it does. Job stands as a witness that even in ashes, worship is possible—and that God remains sovereign over every storm.

REFLECTION

1. What part of Job's example in chapters 1-2 most challenges your understanding of suffering and faith?

2. Why is it important that Scripture calls Job "blameless" before any suffering begins?

3. How do Job's responses in grief (tearing his robe, worshiping, confessing God's sovereignty) shape your view of faithful lament?

4. When have you been tempted to interpret suffering as divine displeasure, and how does Job 1-2 correct that thinking?

5. Which of Job's qualities—integrity, reverence, perseverance—do you most need to cultivate right now?

6. How does knowing that God remained sovereign and present behind the scenes bring comfort in your own trials?

DISCUSSION

1. Why is the heavenly dialogue in Job 1-2 important for understanding the book's message about suffering and righteousness?

2. How does the accuser's question ("Does Job fear God for nothing?") challenge the motives of believers today?

3. What does Job's grief teach us about the place of emotional honesty in the life of a Christian?

4. Why is it significant that Job's suffering had no connection to moral failure?

5. How do Job's wife and Job's friends illustrate both the importance—and danger—of how believers respond to someone else's pain?

6. What lessons can church communities learn from Job 1-2 about supporting those who suffer without making false assumptions?

2

JOB'S LAMENT

JOB 3

Objective: To see that honest lament is a faithful response to deep suffering and an essential part of walking with God.

INTRODUCTION

In 2010, after a devastating earthquake struck Haiti, a team of relief workers gathered in Port-au-Prince to assist survivors. One worker recalled walking through a crowd of people who were singing hymns amid the rubble. But the songs were not triumphant—they were laments. Mothers who had lost children, fathers who had lost homes, and neighbors who had lost entire families stood together singing through tears. One woman was overheard praying, "God, we do not understand. But you are still our God." Her voice cracked under the weight of grief, yet her words rose like incense of sorrowful praise.

Their worship was not neat or composed. It was raw, trembling, and honest—an expression of faith struggling to breathe in the dust of tragedy. They were not denying their pain; they were offering it. Their cries were not polished theology but the language of human hearts refusing to let go of God.

Job's lament in Job 3 sits in that same sacred space. After seven days of silence, his anguish erupts. He does not curse God, but he does curse the day he was born. His sorrow is deep, his questions sharp, his lament unfiltered. Yet even in this darkness, his words are addressed toward God. Job shows Christians that authentic faith does not hide its wounds—faith brings them into the presence of the One who hears.

EXAMINATION

The silence shatters (3:1)

The quiet of Job 2:13 hangs over the opening of Job 3 like a storm ready to break. For seven days, Job's friends sat with him, wordless, while he mourned in ashes. That silence was the only kindness they would offer without qualification. But silence is not a home for long-term suffering; eventually the pressure inside begins to break the vessel. When Job speaks, his words are not polished confessions of trust nor theological reflections. They are raw, unfiltered anguish.

Job "opened his mouth," a phrase that signals deliberation. He is not muttering in delirium; he is speaking intentionally, but from the depths of torment. And he "cursed the day of his birth." Not God. Not himself. But the day that made his suffering possible.

This moment marks a shift from narrative to poetry—from the external, observable story of Job's losses to the internal earthquake of Job's heart. Poetry allows him to say what prose cannot contain. Job's lament is not blasphemy; it is faith with its skin torn off. It is the sound of a believer refusing to hide his pain from the God he still seeks.

Job's curse on the day he was born (3:2–10)

Job directs his curse toward time itself. He wishes his birthday had been swallowed by darkness, reclaimed by chaos, erased from the calendar of creation. Each line is vivid:

- "Let that day perish."
- "Let darkness and deep shadow claim it."
- "Let it not rejoice among the days of the year."

Job is not asking God to reverse history; he is expressing the depth of his despair. In Scripture, darkness is often where order and blessing disappear. Job feels as though his life, once filled with God's gifts, has returned to chaos. His words echo the inverse of Genesis 1: instead of "let there be light," Job pleads for darkness. Instead of creation's order, he longs for unmaking.

This lament is not theological argument but emotional honesty. The righteous are not immune to thoughts like these when suffering becomes unbearable. Job does not advocate nihilism; he simply wonders whether his existence has become too painful to bear.

The key theological point: Job is still speaking to God, not abandoning him. Only believers wrestle like this. Only believers expect a world of meaning. His lament is the cry of a heart that knows God is sovereign and cannot reconcile that sovereignty with his own agony.

Longing for death at birth (3:11–15)

Job's lament shifts into a series of "whys"—a word soaked in pain and longing. "Why did I not die at birth?" "Why did knees receive me?" "Why did breasts nurse me?" He imagines that an early death would have been a mercy. At least then he would have moved quickly from a world of tears into the quiet of the grave.

Ancient Near Eastern people often viewed Sheol as a realm of stillness—a shadowy but peaceful place where turmoil could not reach. Job's longing here is not grounded in Christian eschatology; it is the perspective of a man who wants relief, not annihilation. He is not suicidal in the modern sense; he is exhausted. He is asking why he was preserved for a life that has become unbearable.

In verses 14–15, Job imagines lying with kings and princes in the grave—those who once built cities now silent. This imagery underlines the universal truth that suffering, status, power, and wealth all collapse into the same quiet at death. Suffering has leveled Job's perspective. Death, from his vantage point, looks like rest.

But again, this is lament, not doctrine. Job is not teaching that death is better than life; he is expressing how his particular life now feels.

The grave as rest for the weary (3:16–19)

Job compares himself to a stillborn child—one who never tasted the griefs of life. It is one of the most painful images in Scripture, but Job's purpose is not morbid fascination. He is making the point that death seems kinder than his current reality.

He describes Sheol as a place where "the wicked cease from troubling," the weary rest, and captives finally hear no taskmaster's shout. This meditation is not a doctrinal treatise on the afterlife; it is the voice of a man longing for reprieve. Yet it also reveals something profound about Job's worldview: he believes that God governs both life and death. He does not fear death. *He fears meaningless suffering.*

Job's lament reflects a universal ache—the longing not simply for life to end, but for agony to stop. The church must recognize that Christians may reach these emotional depths without abandoning faith. Honest lament is not rebellion; it is the soul reaching for the God it cannot yet see.

Why give light to those who suffer? (3:20–23)

Here the lament sharpens into a theological question: "Why is light given to him who is in misery?" Job cannot understand why God continues to grant breath to those whose lives have collapsed. From Job's perspective, continued life seems like continued punishment. He is not speaking as a theologian but as a sufferer asking why God sustains what feels unsustainable.

These verses expose a crucial truth about suffering: the deepest wounds are not physical but existential. Job does not ask why his flocks died or why his body is in pain. He asks why God allows the miserable to continue living. This shift from specific grief to universal question marks Job's lament as part of wisdom literature. His pain becomes the lens through which all human sorrow is examined.

Faith has not left him. Only faith asks questions like these. Job assumes God is still involved, still present, still sovereign. But he cannot understand how that sovereignty fits with his agony. His lament is not disbelief but disorientation.

The collapse of peace (3:24–26)

The chapter ends with one of the bleakest declarations in Scripture:

- "Sighing has become my daily food."
- "My groans pour out like water."
- "What I feared has come upon me."
- "I have no peace, no quietness, no rest."

These verses reveal the emotional landscape of suffering. Job is exhausted—spiritually, emotionally, physically. His fears have become his reality. His rest has been replaced by restlessness. His quiet has dissolved into turmoil.

Importantly, Job is not sinning here. The narrator does not rebuke him. God does not condemn him. Lament is permitted. Honest grief does not offend the God who formed our hearts. If anything, Job 3 gives believers permission to bring their deepest sorrows to God without fear of rejection.

Job's lament is not the end of his faith but the beginning of his wrestling. Chapter 3 opens the dialogue that will carry through 35 chapters. Job has not cursed God. He has not abandoned belief. He has acknowledged the truth of his pain and laid it before the only One who can make sense of it.

Job's lament is Scripture's reminder that the faithful suffer, the righteous struggle, and Christians may cry out without losing their reverence. The God who heard Job's lament still hears ours.

APPLICATION

1. Honest lament is an expression of faith

Job's cry in chapter 3 reminds believers that lament is not a failure of faith but a function of it. The righteous are not required to mask their agony or pretend their wounds are small. Job does not curse God; he brings his confusion and despair before him. That is what faith does. Suffering creates pressure that must find a voice, and lament gives form to that struggle without severing trust. Many Christians silence their pain because they fear it sounds unspiritual, but Scripture teaches otherwise. God invites believers to speak from the depths, not just the heights. Honest lament acknowledges that life is broken, we are hurting, and God alone can help. Job's example encourages us to pray with transparency, trusting that God is not threatened by our tears or our questions.

2. The believer's value is not erased by suffering

Job curses the day he was born because his pain has overshadowed his sense of purpose. Many believers have felt the same during seasons of intense grief or depression. But Job 3 must be read in the context of Job 1–2, where God declares Job's worth and integrity before heaven. Suffering can distort perspective, making us forget the value God places on our lives. Pain may lead us to believe our existence is meaningless, but God's testimony remains unchanged. He knows our worth even when we cannot see it. In Christ, Christians find identity rooted not in circumstances but in the Creator's delight. When suffering tempts you to question your value, remember that God affirmed Job before the pain—and affirms you in the same way. Your worth remains intact even when life feels empty.

3. Despair is not the end of devotion

Job's longing for death can unsettle modern readers, but Scripture does not condemn him. These words reflect the emotional depths that even faithful Christians may reach in seasons of unbearable sorrow. Spiritual maturity does not eliminate despair; it anchors us when despair comes. Job's anguish is shaped by faith, not by unbelief. He speaks to God because he still expects God to hear. You may experience seasons when grief crushes joy, when questions drown out comfort, or when exhaustion overshadows hope. These moments do not disqualify you from faith. They reveal that devotion can survive even when confidence shakes. Job shows that despair can coexist with reverence, and questions can coexist with trust. Faith perseveres not because believers feel strong, but because God holds the suffering with compassion and mercy.

4. Suffering calls Christians to community

Suffering often isolates. Pain shrinks the world, and grief convinces us no one understands. Job was surrounded by friends who sat with him in silence before they spoke unwisely. Their presence, however imperfect, illustrates a truth: Christians are not meant to suffer alone. Job's lament makes this clear. He speaks only after seven days of companionship. Even when the friends later fail, their initial presence reflects God's design for comfort. Christians today need communities where lament is welcomed, not silenced. Churches must learn to sit with one another in sorrow, offering compassion instead of explanations. When believers share their burdens, they reflect the character of the God who bears our sorrows. Suffering calls us into deeper fellowship, reminding us that grief is lighter when carried together in the body of Christ.

CONCLUSION

Job 3 brings us into the inner world of a suffering believer. The man who once worshiped through tears now cries out in anguish, not because his faith has failed, but because his pain has overwhelmed him. Job teaches believers that lament is not rebellion—it is relationship. God invites his people to bring their sorrow, confusion, and longing into his presence without pretending that everything is fine. Honest grief becomes part of faithful living.

These raw words prepare us for the long dialogue ahead. Job will wrestle with his friends, with his assumptions, and with God himself. Yet even here, in the darkest chapter of his life, he does not turn away from the Lord. His lament is a beginning, not an end—a step into deeper understanding, not a retreat from faith.

REFLECTION

1. When have you felt the kind of emotional honesty Job expresses in this chapter?

2. Why is it important to remember that lament is not the opposite of faith?

3. What parts of Job's lament resonate most with experiences of suffering you have faced?

4. How does Job 3 challenge assumptions that faithful Christians must always feel hopeful or composed?

5. Where do you most need to bring honest sorrow before God rather than hiding it?

6. How can Job's lament help you respond to others who are in deep pain?

DISCUSSION

1. How does the shift from prose to poetry in Job 3 help us understand the depth of Job's suffering?

2. In what ways does Job's curse on the day of his birth reveal both anguish and lingering faith?

3. Why is it significant that Job never curses God, even in his darkest lament?

4. How should Christians view Job's longing for death in this chapter—with condemnation or compassion? Why?

5. What does Job 3 teach about the importance of giving space and permission for lament in the church?

6. How can congregations create a healthier environment for believers in pain to express sorrow without judgment?

3

EASY ANSWERS TO HARD QUESTIONS

JOB 4–14

Objective: To understand why simplistic explanations fail in the face of suffering and why humble, honest faith is essential.

INTRODUCTION

In 1998, after Hurricane Mitch devastated Honduras, relief workers from around the world poured into the region. One volunteer later recalled sitting with a local minister whose entire congregation had lost homes, livelihoods, and several family members. As they surveyed the wreckage, a well-meaning visitor approached and said, "God must be teaching you something through this." The minister looked down at the mud-soaked ground and replied gently, "Brother, please—do not speak of things you do not understand."

He wasn't denying God's presence or sovereignty. He was responding to a common mistake: the tendency to offer tidy explanations for suffering that is anything but tidy. The visitor wanted to help, but his words added weight to an already unbearable burden. What the minister needed was compassion, not a theory.

Job faced a similar experience. His friends came with good intentions, but their confidence exceeded their understanding. They believed the world worked according to simple spiritual math: righteous people prosper; wicked people suffer. So when Job lamented, they assumed he must be hiding some secret sin. Their theology felt neat—until it collided with Job's reality.

Job 4–14 teaches us that faith requires humility, not certainty. Suffering demands compassion, not premature conclusions. And wisdom listens long before it speaks.

EXAMINATION

When comfort turns into correction (4:1–5:7)

After Job's searing lament in chapter 3, his friends can no longer remain silent. Eliphaz speaks first—not because he is the wisest, but because he is the oldest. His opening words sound gentle, almost sympathetic, but beneath the surface lies a familiar assumption: the righteous do not suffer like this unless they have sinned. Eliphaz reminds Job that he once strengthened others in their trials, and now he should accept correction in his own. His logic is simple: suffering reveals guilt; prosperity reveals righteousness.

Eliphaz's worldview is built on a tidy moral formula—the retribution principle. He believes the world runs on predictable spiritual physics: sow wickedness, reap trouble; sow integrity, reap blessing. So when he sees Job in ruins, he concludes the cause must lie within Job, not beyond him. The trouble is that Eliphaz's theology has no room for innocent suffering. He offers traditional wisdom, but mistimes and misapplies it.

His counsel is not malicious, but it is misguided. He assumes the character of God based on the circumstances of Job. He urges Job to accept discipline and return to God, not realizing Job has already been walking faithfully with him. In Eliphaz, Christians see the danger of oversimplifying the moral structure of the world.

Job's first reply: The pain beneath the theology (6:1–7:21)

Job responds with desperation. His grief, he says, outweighs the sand of the sea. Eliphaz's explanations feel like cold logic laid on a burning heart. Job longs for God to grant him death—not from hatred of life, but from exhaustion. He pleads for his friends to show kindness rather than accusation. Job's honesty exposes what the friends cannot yet grasp: pain distorts perception, multiplies fear, and clouds judgment.

In chapter 7, Job shifts his lament toward God. He does not curse God but questions him boldly: "What is man, that you make so much of him?" His suffering feels relentless, and he wonders why God will not let him rest. Job's questions are not rebellion. They are the cries of a believer struggling to make sense of God's involvement in his pain.

Job's dialogue reveals a crucial truth about suffering: faith wrestles; it does not always resolve quickly. Unlike the friends, Job does not pretend the world is neat. His protest is not faithlessness but faith seeking understanding.

Bildad's defense of tradition (8:1–22)

Bildad speaks next. He is more blunt than Eliphaz and more committed to tradition than compassion. He insists that God is just and therefore Job's children must have sinned. This is one of the most painful missteps in the book, for Bildad assumes moral failure where God has declared innocence.

Bildad represents the kind of believer who values theological systems more than people. He defends God's justice by accusing Job rather than questioning his own assumptions. His worldview is even narrower than Eliphaz's: if Job repents, God will restore him. Bildad's God is predictable, mechanistic, exacting—a God who always rewards and punishes according to human expectations.

The irony is that Bildad's theology is partly correct: God is just. But his application is fatally flawed. He cannot imagine a world where the righteous suffer for reasons unknown. His tradition blinds him to Job's humanity.

Job's second reply: The honesty of bewildered faith (9:1–10:22)

Job agrees that God is just—but the world, as he experiences it, is not tidy. He acknowledges God's power and wisdom, then confesses his inability to understand how his suffering fits within divine justice. Job's speeches in these chapters pulse with tension: he believes God is righteous, yet his own experience feels unjust.

Job does not accuse God of wrongdoing; he simply admits that he cannot reconcile his suffering with what he knows of God's character. This is the heart of biblical lament: bringing contradictions to God without abandoning him.

In chapter 10, Job pleads for God to reveal the reason for his suffering. He feels hunted, scrutinized, crushed. His words are sharp, but they are spoken to God, not about God. Job refuses to surrender the relationship even when he cannot understand it.

Zophar's zeal without understanding (11:1–20)

Zophar is the most rigid of the three friends. He accuses Job of talking too much and knowing too little. He insists that God has punished Job less than he deserves. His answer is simple: Job must repent. The implication is clear—Job's suffering is self-inflicted.

Zophar takes the retribution principle to its harshest extreme. For him, the righteous always prosper, and the wicked always suffer. There is no mystery, no nuance, no hidden dimension. His theology cannot tolerate tension.

Zophar's certainty blinds him to the possibility that Job's suffering is not punishment but a test of faithfulness. His confidence in his own understanding becomes arrogance. In his voice, the book of Job warns Christians against the danger of defending God inaccurately.

Job's final speech in the cycle: Holding to integrity (12:1–14:22)

Job responds with both sorrow and sarcasm. "No doubt you are the people, and wisdom will die with you." He exposes the friends' assumptions and insists on his own integrity: "I know I am blameless." Job never claims sinlessness—only innocence regarding the charges implied by the friends.

In chapter 13, Job appeals directly to God. He is willing to risk rebuke, correction, or judgment, but he cannot accept the simplistic accusations of his friends. His boldness surprises readers, but it is rooted in reverence. Job wants a relationship with God more than he wants an explanation from his friends.

Chapter 14 reveals Job's deepest anguish. Life feels frail, short, and filled with trouble. He pleads for mercy, for space to breathe, for hope beyond the grave. Here Job begins to glimpse a longing that will grow throughout the book—the hope that God might provide vindication beyond this life.

Job ends the first cycle still wounded, still confused, but still speaking to God. His faith is bruised, but not broken.

The theological heart of the first cycle

The first cycle of speeches reveals several crucial truths:

1. **Traditional theology cannot explain every form of suffering.** Eliphaz, Bildad, and Zophar rely on formulas, not wisdom.

2. **The righteous may suffer in ways that contradict human expectations.** Job's experience exposes the limits of the retribution principle.

3. **Lament is a legitimate form of faith.** Job's complaints are spoken in relationship, not rebellion.

4. **God's justice is bigger than human logic.** The friends defend a smaller God than the one who actually exists.

5. **Job holds to integrity even when answers fail.** The test of faith is not whether believers feel strong, but whether they continue seeking God when life makes no sense.

6. **Suffering exposes the difference between simplistic theology and genuine wisdom.** Job wrestles honestly; the friends argue confidently. Job's struggle is closer to truth than their certainty.

The first cycle sets the stage for deeper conflict—and deeper revelation—in the chapters ahead.

APPLICATION

1. Beware of offering tidy answers to untidy suffering

Eliphaz, Bildad, and Zophar prove that even sincere believers can wound others when they cling to simple explanations for complex pain. Their theology was partly true—God is just—but their application was painfully wrong. They assumed suffering always reveals sin and prosperity always reveals righteousness. Christians can fall into the same trap when we speak before listening or diagnose before understanding. Job's friends remind us that truth without compassion distorts God's character and crushes hurting people. When believers offer quick answers—"Everything happens for a reason," "God must be teaching you something," or "You just need more faith"—we risk sounding more like the friends than like Christ. Wisdom listens longer than it speaks. Faithful comfort refuses to shrink human suffering into neat formulas. When we meet someone in pain, our first calling is presence, not explanation.

2. Faith wrestles honestly rather than settling for clichés

Job refuses to accept superficial explanations for his suffering. His friends offer ready-made answers, but Job insists on honesty—even when that honesty leads him into painful questions. He knows God is just, yet his situation feels unjust. Instead of pretending, he wrestles. This is not weakness but mature faith. Christians sometimes believe they must silence their questions to appear faithful, but Scripture invites us to bring those questions to God. Job shows that God honors the believer who seeks him in confusion rather than the one who pretends to understand what he does not. Real faith does not hide struggle behind clichés; it presses into God even when clarity seems distant. Wrestling is not the opposite of trust—it is often the path toward deeper trust.

3. Defending God inaccurately dishonors him

The friends thought they were protecting God's reputation by insisting that suffering must reflect personal sin. But their narrow theology painted a picture of God that was smaller, colder, and harsher than the God Job knew. When Christians claim to know exactly why someone suffers or insist that God always acts according to predictable patterns, we risk doing the same. We misrepresent God when we speak where he has not spoken or declare certainty where Scripture allows mystery. Job teaches believers to guard God's character by refusing to reduce him to our systems. God remains sovereign, just, and compassionate—even when the world appears chaotic. Our task is not to defend simplistic ideas about God but to honor the fullness of who he is. Humility is better theology than certainty when certainty has no foundation.

4. Integrity matters more than explanations

Job's friends wanted answers; Job wanted God. He held to his integrity even when he could not make sense of his suffering. This is the heart of faith—seeking God when explanations fail. Christians often long for reasons, but Scripture teaches that obedience is not built on understanding; it is built on trust. Job reminds us that maintaining integrity is more important than resolving every question. In seasons of confusion, believers may not know why something happens, but they still know who God is. That is enough to sustain faith. The greatest victories in suffering often occur not when circumstances improve, but when we cling to righteousness despite confusion. Job's endurance shows that integrity anchored in reverence is stronger than any storm. Our calling is to walk faithfully with God even when the path makes no sense.

CONCLUSION

The first cycle of speeches reveals the tension at the heart of the book of Job. The friends cling to a tidy world where righteousness always leads to blessing and suffering always signals sin. Job, however, knows from experience that life is not that simple. His integrity stands firm even as his questions intensify. He refuses to surrender either his faith or his honesty.

These chapters teach believers that wisdom is not found in quick answers but in courageous trust. God is too great to be reduced to formulas, and suffering is too complex to be explained with clichés. Job's faith is bruised but alive—seeking God even when his world makes no sense. As the dialogue unfolds, the friends' confidence will weaken while Job's longing for God deepens. The real victory here is not in understanding suffering but in remaining faithful through it.

REFLECTION

1. Why do you think Job's friends felt so confident in their explanations of his suffering?

2. When have you been tempted to offer quick answers instead of patient compassion to someone in pain?

3. How does Job's honest wrestling encourage you to bring your own questions before God?

4. What parts of the first cycle resonate with experiences you've had with unhelpful or hurtful counsel?

5. Where do you see yourself more in Job—and where do you see yourself in the friends?

6. How can this section help you respond more wisely to suffering in your family, friendships, or congregation?

DISCUSSION

1. Why is the retribution principle so appealing, and why does the book of Job challenge its simplicity?

2. How does Job's refusal to accept easy answers demonstrate both humility and courage?

3. In what ways do Eliphaz, Bildad, and Zophar represent sincere but misguided attempts to defend God?

4. How does Job 4–14 help us understand the difference between theological truth and pastoral wisdom?

5. Why is it important to acknowledge mystery in the face of suffering rather than forcing explanations?

6. What would it look like for your congregation to become a community where lament, questions, and compassion are welcomed rather than silenced?

4

WHEN FRIENDS WOUND
JOB 15-21

Objective: To recognize how rigid, oversimplified theology can wound the suffering and to learn compassion that reflects God's wisdom.

INTRODUCTION

In 2013, after the Boston Marathon bombing, hospitals filled with victims whose lives had changed in an instant. One survivor, Rebekah Gregory, later described sitting in her hospital bed listening to visitors try to make sense of the tragedy. Some offered comfort; others offered explanations. One well-meaning acquaintance told her, "God must have spared you because he knew you'd be strong enough to handle this." Rebekah later wrote that those words, though kindly meant, felt like salt in a wound. She didn't feel strong. She didn't feel chosen. She felt broken—and explanations did not ease the pain.

What she needed most was compassion, presence, and patience. Not theories. Not formulas. Not guesses about God's purposes. She needed someone to sit with her in the ache.

Job needed the same. But in Job 15-21, his friends shifted from comforters to critics. Their theology grew sharper than their empathy. They believed in a tidy moral universe where good people prosper and bad people suffer—and because Job suffered, they concluded he must be hiding sin. Their certainty wounded more deeply than their silence ever had.

The second cycle of speeches teaches believers a difficult truth: good intentions can become harmful when we value explanations more than compassion. Sometimes the most faithful response to suffering is not to solve it, but to sit with it.

EXAMINATION

The tightening grip of retribution theology (15:1–16)

When the second cycle begins, Eliphaz is no longer gentle. In the first cycle he wrapped his assumptions in courtesy; in this cycle, he strips away all restraint. Job's lament in chapter 14—his cry for compassion, his longing for a mediator—has offended the friends' moral instincts. So Eliphaz responds sharply: Job's words are "windy," his arguments dangerous, his tone rebellious. The implication is clear: Job's pain has driven him into spiritual arrogance.

Eliphaz's theology has not changed; it has hardened. He still believes suffering always reveals sin. Job must be concealing something, refusing correction, or resisting God. Eliphaz describes the wicked in ways that unmistakably point at Job—trembling with fear, wracked with anguish, losing their possessions, dwelling in darkness. His speech is less comfort than indictment.

This moment reveals an uncomfortable truth: when people cling to rigid beliefs about how God must act, they often prioritize their system over compassion. Eliphaz is more committed to defending his worldview than understanding Job's pain. In his view, suffering threatens the moral order, so Job must be corrected, even crushed, to preserve that order.

Eliphaz's approach warns believers that good theology can be misused when divorced from humility and relationship. Truth delivered without tenderness becomes a weapon.

Job's reply: Suffering as lived experience, not theory (16:1–17)

Job responds with one of the most painful speeches in the book. "Miserable comforters are you all." His friends have not relieved his grief; they have multiplied it. Their words sting because they imply that Job's agony is self-inflicted.

Job describes how he feels before God—struck, crushed, battered, besieged. His imagery is graphic, not because Job believes God is malicious, but because his pain is overwhelming. His lament remains anchored in faith; he speaks to God and about God because he still believes God is central to his life. Job is not turning away; he is reaching out from the depths.

This section reveals a key truth for Christians: pain experienced is never as simple as pain explained. Job knows his suffering from the inside, while the friends interpret it from the outside. His experience refuses to fit into their categories, and his honesty challenges their assumptions.

Even in agony, Job insists on his integrity. He has not sinned in ways that justify his suffering. He will not lie to comfort his friends' worldview. His faith, though battered, refuses to collapse.

A longing for a witness in heaven (16:18–17:16)

Job's greatest heartbreak is not physical suffering but divine silence. He longs for someone in heaven to plead his case—someone who sees his innocence and can mediate between him and God. This longing anticipates the hope that will grow later: a heavenly advocate, a redeemer who can stand for him.

He imagines such a witness appealing to God on his behalf: "my witness is in heaven." This is not a rejection of God but a yearning for God to reveal himself with clarity and compassion. Job wants someone who can bridge the gap between his human confusion and divine wisdom.

Job's vision here is incomplete, but it anticipates the fuller revelation of Christ as mediator. His instinct is true even if his understanding is partial.

His friends, meanwhile, feel like tormentors. Job believes he will soon die, and he asks who will stand with him then. His grief deepens because the very people who should offer comfort have become agents of pain.

Bildad's escalation: The wicked condemned (18:1–21)

Bildad's second speech is harsher than his first. He accuses Job of treating them like fools and insists that the wicked suffer precisely as Job is suffering. His speech is vivid: the light of the wicked is extinguished, their steps falter, their traps spring shut, their memory perishes.

All of this is meant to frighten Job into admitting wrongdoing. Bildad's theology cannot allow righteous suffering, so he redraws the lines until Job fits the outline of the wicked.

Bildad's speech illustrates the danger of moral imagination fueled by suspicion. When believers assume guilt without evidence, they distort justice and harm the innocent. Bildad mistakes volume and confidence for truth.

Job's second reply: Hope against hopelessness (19:1–22)

Job responds with one of the most emotionally charged speeches in Scripture. He feels crushed by God and abandoned by people. Family members avoid him. Servants ignore him. Children mock him. Even his wife recoils from him. Job has become a stranger in his own home and an outcast among his community.

Yet amid devastation, a spark of hope blazes: "I know that my redeemer lives." This is not a full New Testament picture of resurrection or Christ, but it is a profound expression of faith. Job believes that someone—God himself, or a representative of God—will one day stand and vindicate him. His hope is not in earthly explanations but in divine justice.

Job's confidence is remarkable. He sees no evidence that God is acting on his behalf, yet he believes vindication will come. His faith shines brightest when his world is darkest.

Zophar's anger and the caricature of wickedness (20:1–29)

Zophar's second speech intensifies the attack. He is offended that Job dares to protest innocence. In Zophar's view, the wicked experience fleeting pleasure but inevitable downfall. Every description of the wicked—from stolen sweetness turning to poison, to wealth evaporating, to terror overwhelming—mirrors Job's condition.

Zophar's rhetoric is cruel, but it reveals a deeper anxiety. If Job is innocent, then their entire theology must be reexamined. It is easier to condemn Job than reconsider their beliefs. Zophar defends his system, not God, and certainly not Job.

His speech represents an approach to suffering rooted in fear rather than compassion—fear that the world may be more complex than his theology allows.

Job's final reply: The stubborn mystery of suffering (21:1–34)

Job dismantles the friends' assumptions with careful observation. The wicked often prosper. They enjoy long lives, numerous children, and abundant success. They die in peace. Meanwhile, the righteous suffer without clear cause. Job is not reversing the retribution principle; he is exposing its limits.

He insists that life does not always reflect moral accounting in obvious ways. God's justice is real, but its outworking remains hidden. Job refuses to pretend he knows what he does not know.

He challenges the friends to face the world as it actually is, not as they want it to be. Their neat theology cannot explain the messy reality of human life. Job's willingness to name this mystery is an act of courageous faith.

The second cycle ends with tension unresolved. The friends become more rigid; Job becomes more honest. Their certainty grows thinner; his hope grows deeper. The stage is set for the final and most heated cycle.

APPLICATION

1. Compassion must shape our theology, not the other way around

The great failure of Job's friends is not that their theology is entirely wrong but that it is applied without compassion. They cling to a system that explains suffering neatly, but life is not neat. When believers force others into rigid categories—"you must have sinned," "you must deserve this," "God is teaching you something"—we trade empathy for certainty. Job's friends cared more about defending their assumptions than comforting their companion. Christians today face the same temptation. When we value being right more than being loving, we misrepresent God's heart. True wisdom begins with compassion. Theology must guide us, but it must never harden us. God calls his people to speak truth with tenderness, to hold convictions with humility, and to be present with the wounded before proclaiming answers. Compassion shapes faithful counsel; certainty alone often wounds.

2. Faith endures even when God feels distant

Job's cries in this cycle are raw and unfiltered, yet they are addressed toward God. He feels abandoned, unheard, and crushed, but he refuses to sever the relationship. His faith is not expressed in confident declarations but in persistent lament. Many Christians assume faith must always sound strong or hopeful. Job teaches otherwise. Faith sometimes sounds like confusion, protest, or groaning. The strength of faith lies not in how polished it appears but in its refusal to walk away from God when he feels far. Christians may face seasons when prayer feels one-sided and God seems silent. Job's example encourages us to keep seeking, keep speaking, and keep trusting—even when emotions rebel. God honors the believer who remains in the struggle. Faith's endurance is often revealed not in victory, but in perseverance through darkness.

3. Bad counsel often comes from good intentions

Eliphaz, Bildad, and Zophar did not set out to harm Job. They came with intentions to comfort, but their commitment to a rigid worldview made them blind to his pain. Christians today can fall into the same trap. We want to help, but we speak before understanding. We quote Scripture without context. We prescribe solutions before listening to wounds. The friends' speeches warn us that sincere motives do not erase harmful effects. Good intentions must be partnered with humility, patience, and discernment. Before we speak into someone's suffering, we should ask: Have I listened long enough? Have I prayed for wisdom? Am I more focused on helping them or protecting my beliefs? True comfort requires entering another's pain, not explaining it from a safe distance.

4. Hope grows even in wounded hearts

Job's declaration, "I know that my redeemer lives," bursts forth in the middle of his deepest despair. His world has collapsed; his friends have become accusers; and God remains silent. Yet something stubborn and holy rises within him—a conviction that God will vindicate him. Job's hope does not rest on circumstances but on the character of God. For believers today, this is a lifeline. Hope is not optimism; it is trust in the God who sees, knows, and remembers even when we feel forgotten. Christians can cultivate hope not by denying their wounds but by anchoring their hearts in God's faithfulness. Suffering may bruise us, but it cannot extinguish the hope God plants within us. Job teaches us that even when everything else is stripped away, hope can survive—and sometimes shine even brighter.

CONCLUSION

The second cycle of speeches exposes the widening gap between Job's experience and the friends' certainty. Their belief in a simple moral universe demands that Job must be at fault, but his integrity and his anguish tell another story. Instead of softening, their explanations harden; instead of comforting, they condemn. Job, however, continues to wrestle honestly with God. His questions deepen, his pain intensifies, and his isolation grows—but so does his hope.

These chapters remind Christians that wisdom requires humility, not quick conclusions. God's world is more complex than the friends' formulas allow, and suffering often defies human explanation. The faithful path is not to force clarity where God has left mystery, but to walk with compassion, patience, and reverence. Job's hope in a living redeemer rises from the ashes of misunderstanding, teaching Christians that even when others wound us, God remains near.

REFLECTION

1. When have you experienced the pain of being misunderstood or misjudged during suffering?

2. How does Job's honesty in these chapters challenge the way you think about expressing grief to God?

3. Why do you think the friends became more rigid and accusatory over time instead of more compassionate?

4. Which parts of Job's responses resonate most with your own experience of wrestling with God?

5. How does Job's declaration, "I know that my redeemer lives," strengthen your understanding of hope?

6. What steps can you take to become a wiser, more compassionate presence when others are hurting?

DISCUSSION

1. Why is the retribution principle so deeply rooted in the thinking of Job's friends—and often in Christians today?

2. How does Job 15–21 demonstrate the difference between "correct theology" and "rightly applied theology"?

3. In what ways does Job challenge the assumption that suffering ought to produce silence or stoicism?

4. What dangers emerge when we prioritize defending our theological frameworks over understanding someone's pain?

5. How can the church cultivate a community where believers can express deep sorrow without fear of judgment?

6. What does Job's persistent hope teach us about trusting God when circumstances seem to deny his care?

5

THE LIMITS OF HUMAN WISDOM
JOB 22-27

Objective: To understand that human wisdom is limited, and true faith clings to integrity and humility when explanations fail.

INTRODUCTION

In 1994, Southwest Airlines Flight 1248 experienced a severe mechanical issue shortly after takeoff. The plane shuddered, alarms sounded, and the cabin filled with fear. One passenger recalled watching a fellow traveler confidently explain to everyone around him what was happening: "It's just a pressure adjustment. This is completely normal." Moments later, the pilot announced an emergency landing. The confident passenger's explanation—sincere though it was—had been entirely wrong. He meant to calm people, but his certainty only made the fear and confusion worse.

His mistake wasn't malice. It was assumption. He wanted the world to fit his understanding, and he spoke as though it did. But reality refused to cooperate.

Job's friends make the same error in Job 22–27. Their explanations are spoken with absolute certainty, but their certainty is misplaced. They assume suffering always exposes sin and prosperity always proves righteousness. When Job's experience contradicts their system, they cling to their assumptions rather than reconsider their worldview. They speak confidently but wrongly—and their misplaced confidence wounds rather than comforts.

The third cycle of speeches shows how human wisdom collapses when it cannot accommodate the complexity of real suffering. Job, meanwhile, refuses easy answers and holds fast to integrity. His honesty becomes wisdom, while their certainty reveals its limits.

EXAMINATION

Eliphaz's final speech: Accusation replacing compassion (22:1–30)

The third cycle begins with a bookend of harsh certainty. Eliphaz—who once spoke as a cautious counselor—now speaks as a prosecutor. His words no longer hint at Job's guilt; they declare it explicitly. He claims Job has exploited the poor, ignored widows, withheld water from the thirsty, and turned the vulnerable away empty-handed. These accusations are invented out of thin air. Nothing in the narrative supports them.

Why does Eliphaz resort to fabrication? Because his worldview is collapsing. If Job is innocent, his retribution-based theology cannot stand. Rather than reconsidering his assumptions, Eliphaz reshapes reality to preserve them. He cannot accept a righteous sufferer, so Job must be reimagined as wicked. It is easier to condemn a friend than to reexamine cherished beliefs.

Eliphaz's speech shows how rigid systems can twist faith into falsehood. Without compassion, theology becomes weaponized. Without humility, wisdom becomes presumption. Eliphaz ends with a call for Job to repent and be restored—a formulaic promise that ignores everything the prologue has revealed.

The lesson is sobering: when belief in a tidy moral universe matters more than truth or relationship, even sincere believers may bear false witness in God's name.

Job's reply: Integrity in the face of slander (23:1–17)

Job responds not with anger but with longing. He wants to find God—to bring his case before the divine throne where justice is uncorrupted. He is convinced that if he could stand before God, he would be vindicated. Job is not seeking escape from suffering; he is seeking truth.

Chapter 23 is one of the most intimate windows into Job's heart. He admits he cannot locate God. He searches east and west, north and south, but God remains hidden. Yet Job's confidence remains: "He knows the way that I take; when he has tried me, I shall come out as gold."

Job's integrity is not self-righteousness—it is courageous honesty. He refuses to confess sins he has not committed simply to satisfy the friends or quiet his own anguish. Job models a faith that holds fast to moral integrity even when suffering makes obedience seem pointless.

At the same time, Job acknowledges the fear and trembling that accompany God's hiddenness. God's silence unnerves him, but it does not unseat his faith.

The terror of divine mystery (24:1–25)

Job's reflections turn outward: if God is just, why does injustice flourish? Why are the poor neglected, the fatherless crushed, and the wicked allowed to prosper? Job does not challenge God's righteousness; he challenges the friends' simplistic understanding of it.

He observes what the friends refuse to see: the world is morally complex. Evil often goes unpunished, and the oppressed often remain unheard. Job's observations are not cynical—they are realistic. He is not denying divine sovereignty; he is confessing human limitation.

Job's critique exposes the friends' denial of reality. Their tidy theology cannot explain the world Job sees. Their moral formulas collapse under the weight of lived experience.

The irony is that Job, the one suffering most, is the one who sees the world most clearly. Pain has sharpened his perception, not dulled it.

Bildad's final speech: The shortest and weakest (25:1–6)

Bildad speaks next—but he barely speaks at all. His final speech is only six verses, and its content is thin. He repeats an argument already made several times: humans are impure compared to God, so how can anyone claim innocence?

Bildad's brevity reveals exhaustion. The friends have run out of arguments. Their system has no flexibility, no nuance, no capacity for mystery. When confronted with Job's integrity and empirical reality, their theology simply stalls.

Bildad's final claim is technically true—God is holy and transcendent—but misapplied. Job never claimed sinless perfection, only innocence regarding the charges implied by his suffering. Bildad answers a question Job never asked.

This is what happens when arguments outlast empathy: once-compassionate friends become echo chambers of cliché.

Job's closing words: Defiance, dignity, and disciplined reverence (26:1–14)

Chapter 26 contains one of the most theologically profound speeches in the book. Job responds to Bildad with a sweeping vision of God's greatness. He describes God's power over the earth, the seas, the heavens, and the underworld. He portrays God as sovereign over creation in ways the friends have never even imagined.

Yet Job concludes with a stunning insight: "These are but the outskirts of his ways, and how small a whisper do we hear of him!" In other words: *Everything we know about God is only the edge of the truth.*

This is Job's turning point. His suffering has not diminished his awe—it has deepened it. Job humbly acknowledges that divine wisdom exceeds human comprehension.

Ironically, Job—whom the friends accuse of irreverence—offers the most exalted understanding of God so far.

Job's oath of innocence (27:1–6)

Job ends the third cycle with a solemn vow. He swears by the living God—whom he says has made his life bitter—that he will not lie to satisfy his accusers. He will not renounce his integrity. He will not pretend to be guilty when he is not.

His insistence is not pride; it is faithfulness. Job refuses to confess sins he has not committed because doing so would be dishonest before God. His integrity is an act of worship, not self-defense.

He adds that the wicked truly do suffer in the long run, but he insists that this pattern cannot be used to diagnose individual cases. Job's view is more nuanced than the friends' black-and-white system.

Job's final speech closes the cycle with clarity: human wisdom is partial, God's ways are vast, integrity matters more than easy answers, and simplistic theology cannot bear the weight of real suffering

The third cycle ends where the friends began—but Job has moved forward. Their certainty has shriveled; his wisdom has expanded. Their theology has collapsed; his hope persists.

The groundwork is now laid for the magnificent wisdom poem of chapter 28 and the arrival of Elihu.

APPLICATION

1. Humility must guide our theology, especially when we face mystery

The third cycle exposes a painful truth: when believers cling to rigid theological systems, they may speak confidently while understanding little. Eliphaz, Bildad, and Zophar defend a simplified view of God because they cannot bear a world where the righteous suffer without explanation. But their certainty blinds them to compassion, and their theology shrinks God rather than exalting him. Job, on the other hand, acknowledges mystery. He knows God is just, but he also knows human wisdom cannot map every corner of divine purpose. His humility becomes a model for Christians learning to live with unanswered questions. Faith does not require us to solve every part of God's governance; it calls us to trust the God whose wisdom surpasses our own. Humility is the gateway to reverence, and reverence protects us from harming others with shallow certainties.

2. Integrity matters even when accusations feel overwhelming

Job refuses to confess sins he has not committed—not out of pride, but out of devotion to truth. For many Christians today, suffering brings pressure to question their own integrity or accept false guilt imposed by others. Job shows that faithfulness includes holding fast to righteousness even when others misjudge us. He does not claim perfection, only honesty. Christians facing unjust criticism, relational strain, or false assumptions can learn from Job's resolve. Integrity is not negotiable, and it is not dependent on human approval. It is the fruit of a heart set on pleasing God. Job teaches that honest, God-centered living sustains believers even when circumstances and voices around them distort the story. Integrity grounded in reverence becomes an anchor when external explanations crumble.

3. The world is more complex than simple formulas can explain

Job observes realities the friends refuse to acknowledge: the wicked sometimes prosper, the righteous sometimes suffer, and the moral patterns of the world do not always appear immediately on the surface. His insights challenge Christians to resist simplistic interpretations of suffering—whether our own or others'. Faith does not eliminate complexity; it helps us navigate it with honesty and compassion. Many spiritual wounds occur when Christians try to force life into neat categories that Scripture itself does not support. Job invites us to embrace the tension between divine justice and human experience without abandoning trust in God's goodness. Wisdom grows when we acknowledge complexity and refuse to let reductionist explanations replace genuine engagement with life's mysteries.

4. God's greatness exceeds our explanations—and that is good news

Job's vision of God in chapter 26 is breathtaking. He sees God's power in creation, his mastery over chaos, his sovereignty over life and death—and then concludes that all this represents only "the outskirts" of God's ways. This perspective transforms suffering. A God this vast cannot be reduced to formulas. His purposes cannot be contained by human expectations. While this may unsettle us, it also comforts us. A small, controllable god could never sustain us through deep suffering, but the God Job describes—sovereign, wise, and beyond comprehension—can. Christians can face the unknown because they trust the One who knows all things. Job reminds us that God's greatness is not a threat to faith but the foundation of peace amid sorrow and mystery.

CONCLUSION

The third cycle brings the friends' theology to its breaking point. Their once-confident explanations fragment under the weight of Job's innocence and experience. Instead of reconsidering their assumptions, they tighten their grip on a worldview too small for the complexity of life. Their certainty becomes accusation; their counsel becomes harm. They defend God inaccurately and wound their friend unintentionally.

Job, however, moves in the opposite direction. His integrity holds. His longing for God deepens. His honesty sharpens his understanding rather than clouding it. And his vision of God expands beyond simple categories into awe-filled reverence. Job shows that faith does not collapse when answers disappear—it strengthens when it trusts God's wisdom over human systems.

As the cycle closes, the friends are out of words, but Job is not out of hope. The stage is set for the poem on wisdom and the arrival of Elihu. The limits of human wisdom have been exposed—and the need for divine wisdom has never been clearer.

REFLECTION

1. What part of the friends' rigid theology do you most recognize in yourself or in modern church culture?

2. How does Job's humility in the face of mystery challenge your assumptions about God's ways?

3. When have you felt pressure to explain suffering—your own or someone else's—before truly listening?

4. What does Job teach you about maintaining integrity when your circumstances seem to contradict your character?

5. How does Job 22–27 deepen your understanding of the limits of human wisdom?

6. Where do you most need to accept mystery rather than force certainty in your walk with God?

DISCUSSION

1. Why do you think Eliphaz resorts to false accusations in this cycle? What fear drives him?

2. How does Job's insistence on both God's justice and the world's complexity expose the flaws in the friends' worldview?

3. In what ways is Bildad's short final speech a sign that their system has collapsed?

4. How does chapter 26 reshape our understanding of God's greatness and the limits of human explanations?

5. Why is Job's refusal to confess imaginary sins an important model for believers facing unjust criticism?

6. How can churches create healthier spaces where people can wrestle honestly with suffering without fear of being labeled unfaithful?

6

WISDOM'S VOICE
JOB 28

Objective: To learn that true wisdom belongs to God alone and is found through reverent trust, not human explanation.

INTRODUCTION

In 1901, engineers drilling near Beaumont, Texas struck what would become known as the Spindletop gusher. For months, they had searched for oil based on surveys, maps, and geological guesswork. But when the drill hit a pressurized salt dome far beneath the surface, the ground erupted with a geyser of oil shooting more than a hundred feet into the air. Newspapers marveled that the discovery "rewrote the understanding of the earth beneath our feet."

What stunned the experts was not simply the size of the oil field, but how wrong their assumptions had been. Decades of drilling in other places had produced little, yet Spindletop exploded with abundance. Geologists later admitted they had underestimated the region's complexity. Despite their skill, they could not see what lay deep underground. Human knowledge was real—but limited.

Job 28 speaks into that same reality. Job and his friends have dug deep into their experiences, their traditions, and their observations. They have searched for explanations with the same energy as miners searching for treasure. But the mystery of Job's suffering lies far deeper than human wisdom can reach.

Before God answers from the whirlwind, this chapter reminds believers that true wisdom is not discovered by digging harder, arguing longer, or thinking smarter. Wisdom belongs to God alone—and he reveals it not through speculation, but through reverent trust.

EXAMINATION

A sudden change in tone

Job 28 interrupts the back-and-forth argument between Job and his friends with a poem of unexpected beauty and calm. After chapters filled with accusation, lament, sarcasm, and rising tension, this chapter speaks with a measured, contemplative voice. Whether the speaker is Job or an inspired narrator, the effect is the same: the debate pauses so the reader can step back and behold the larger question—*Where can true wisdom be found?*

This is the question Job and his friends have been circling without naming. Job suffers and wants to understand why. The friends defend their system and assume understanding is within reach. But both sides have reached the limits of their knowledge. Wisdom has not emerged from their speeches. Their arguments reveal emotion, conviction, and experience—but not clarity. Job 28 exposes the inadequacy of all human attempts to explain the deep things of God.

This chapter becomes the hinge of the entire book—everything before has shown the failure of human wisdom; everything after will reveal divine wisdom.

Human skill and human limits (28:1–11)

The poem opens with a celebration of human ingenuity. People mine deep into the earth, carving tunnels through rock, dragging precious metals from hidden places, discovering what no animal eye has seen. The imagery is vivid: shafts dug into darkness, men suspended by ropes, lamps piercing underground caverns. Humans uncover silver, gold, iron, copper, and gemstones. Nothing seems out of reach.

This is not cynical; it acknowledges the remarkable creativity God has given humanity. We reshape landscapes, harness resources, and explore places no creature can reach. Even the friends' arguments echo this confidence—they assume wisdom is something humans can dig up through logic, tradition, or observation.

Yet the poem reveals a striking contrast: *humans can find precious metals, but they cannot find wisdom.* The greatest feats of knowledge cannot uncover the moral structure of the universe. Exploration can reach the depths of the earth, but not the depths of God's purposes. Human brilliance stops at the threshold of divine understanding. Job 28 shows that suffering exposes this limit. Job and his friends have been digging, but their shovels cannot reach wisdom's hidden vein.

Wisdom cannot be bought, mined, or traded (28:12–19)

The poem asks again: "But where shall wisdom be found?" Having shown where humans can search, it now shows what wisdom is not. It cannot be purchased with gold. It cannot be traded for precious stones. It cannot be valued in gemstones, onyx, sapphire, coral, quartz, or pearls. Even gold from Ophir is insufficient.

This list is not random; it mirrors the same elements humans extract from the earth. The poet is saying: *the things we prize most highly are worthless when compared to wisdom.*

The friends believed wisdom was within reach—they simply needed to apply their theology correctly. Job believed wisdom existed but remained hidden from him because of his suffering. Job 28 exposes both assumptions. Wisdom is not something humans can acquire the way they acquire wealth or knowledge. It cannot be mastered, purchased, or achieved. It is beyond human effort, skill, and intellect. This is not meant to discourage but to humble. Wisdom is not a possession; it is a gift.

Wisdom is hidden from creation (28:20–22)

The search for wisdom now expands beyond humanity. The poet asks whether creation itself knows the secret. Do the deep places know? Do the oceans? Do destruction and death? Each replies, "We have heard a rumor of it." They sense wisdom's existence, but they do not possess it.

This reveals two truths: (1) Wisdom permeates the world because God has structured creation with order. (2) Yet wisdom itself—the divine understanding behind that order—remains inaccessible.

Suffering heightens this tension. Job has seen the world's beauty and its brokenness. His friends have seen patterns that often hold true but fail in his case. Job 28 teaches that wisdom is not encoded in nature the way minerals are. Observing the world can teach us much, but it cannot reveal God's hidden purposes. Creation reflects wisdom, but cannot explain it.

God alone knows wisdom's way (28:23–27)

The turning point comes in verse 23: "God understands the way to it, and he knows its place." Human hands can dig deep, but only divine eyes see the entirety of creation. God knows wisdom because he made it. The poem roots wisdom in God's actions:

- God looks to the ends of the earth.
- God establishes the force of wind.
- God sets boundaries for waters.
- God decrees the course of rain and lightning.

    These are not random meteorological examples. They show that wisdom is woven into the fabric of creation—the order, balance, and restraint that govern nature. Wisdom is God's because the world is God's.

    Verse 27 is crucial: God "saw it," "declared it," "established it," and "searched it out." These verbs show ownership, revelation, and mastery. Job 28 affirms that wisdom is not chaotic or uncertain. It is grounded in God's character and activity.

    Yet—and this is critical—God does not reveal the mechanisms of wisdom to humanity. He reveals the path of wisdom. Humans cannot see what God sees, but they can walk where God directs.

The revelation of true wisdom: Fear God, turn from evil (28:28)

The poem concludes with one of the most profound summaries in Scripture: "Behold, the fear of the Lord, that is wisdom, and to turn away from evil is understanding."

    This is not resignation; it is revelation. God does not give us exhaustive knowledge of the world's inner workings. He does not explain every instance of suffering. Instead, he gives us the wisdom that matters for daily living.

True wisdom is relational, not speculative. It doesn't begin with answers—it begins with reverence.

"Fear of the Lord" is not terror; it is awe-filled devotion. It is the posture of humility that recognizes God's greatness and humanity's limits. It is the disposition that says, "God knows more than I do, and I trust him." "Turning from evil" is the practical side of wisdom. It is the lived expression of reverence. Wisdom is not proven by explanation but by obedience.

This final verse reframes the entire debate:

- The friends sought wisdom through accusation.
- Job sought wisdom through experience.
- God grounds wisdom in relationship and righteousness.

Job 28 whispers that the answer Job wants will not come in the form he expects. Wisdom will not solve the mystery of suffering; it will call him to trust the God who governs beyond human sight.

Why this poem matters now

Job 28 prepares the reader for what is coming. The friends have exhausted their understanding. Job has exhausted his frustration. Creation itself cannot answer the "why" of suffering. But God will speak soon—and when he does, he will not explain suffering. He will reveal himself.

Job 28 teaches that the wisdom we need most is not the wisdom to interpret suffering, but the wisdom to trust God while suffering remains unexplained.

This chapter stands at the center of the book to remind believers of three truths: (1) Human wisdom is real but limited. (2) God's wisdom is infinite and foundational to creation. (3) The path of wisdom is accessible: fear God, turn from evil.

The poem does not end the book's tension—God will do that. But it does reshape Job's expectations and the reader's perspective. Before God speaks, wisdom must speak—not to explain, but to redirect. Job has cried out for answers. Job 28 responds with a different kind of gift—the call to humility, reverence, and obedience. This is the wisdom Christians walk by when explanations fail.

APPLICATION

1. Wisdom begins with humility before it grows into understanding

Job 28 shows that the first step toward true wisdom is admitting how little we know. Humans can dig tunnels into mountains, probe the depths of the sea, and uncover treasures hidden for millennia. Yet we cannot uncover the deepest purposes of God through intellect, experience, or argument. This humbling truth protects believers from the arrogance that shaped Job's friends. We do not need to grasp everything God is doing to trust that he is wise in all he does. When suffering confronts us with unanswered questions, humility becomes the foundation of faith—not weakness, but strength. Christians who accept their limits gain freedom from the pressure to explain the inexplicable. Wisdom grows as we stop demanding exhaustive answers and begin acknowledging that God's wisdom is enough, even when ours is not.

2. The world reveals God's wisdom, but only God reveals its meaning

Job 28 celebrates the order and beauty of creation. From the paths of lightning to the boundaries of the sea, everything reflects God's wisdom. But the poem insists that creation alone cannot reveal the deep purposes behind God's governance. Believers today often search for meaning in patterns, circumstances, or nature itself. Yet Scripture teaches that only God fully understands the wisdom woven into the universe. When life seems chaotic or unjust, Christians must resist the temptation to read too much into events or draw conclusions the Bible does not support. Instead, we anchor ourselves in the God who sees what we cannot see. Creation testifies to his wisdom; Scripture reveals his will; obedience expresses our trust. God invites us to marvel at his world without assuming we can interpret every detail of his providence.

3. The wisdom God reveals is moral, not exhaustive

Job 28 ends with a simple but profound truth: "the fear of the Lord—that is wisdom, and to turn from evil is understanding." God has not given us the ability to decode every mystery of suffering. Instead, he has given us the wisdom needed to live righteously within those mysteries. This is good news. We do not need to understand why every trial happens to remain faithful through it. The wisdom God reveals directs our character, not our calculations. It calls Christians to reverence, repentance, purity, and obedience. Suffering therefore becomes not a puzzle to solve but a context in which wisdom is practiced. The friends lacked this understanding—they pursued answers instead of righteousness. Job 28 redirects believers toward the wisdom God actually provides: a life shaped by holiness, humility, and the fear of the Lord.

4. Trusting God is the wisest response when life makes no sense

God alone "knows the way to wisdom," and he alone "declared it and searched it out." These phrases ground believers in the truth that God fully understands what we only glimpse. When suffering, confusion, or injustice strike, the wisest response is not frantic searching but steadfast trust. Wisdom finds rest in God's character rather than in explanations. This is especially important for Christians facing prolonged trials, unanswered prayers, or circumstances that defy moral logic. Trust does not eliminate grief, but it anchors the heart in the One who governs the universe with perfect wisdom. Job 28 assures us that the God who built the foundations of the earth is not confused by our circumstances. When we cannot trace his hand, we still trust his wisdom, walk in his ways, and wait in his presence. That is the essence of biblical wisdom.

CONCLUSION

Job 28 stands like a quiet mountain peak in the middle of a stormy landscape. Job and his friends have dug through every argument they know, yet none of them has uncovered the meaning of Job's suffering. Their words reveal intelligence, passion, and conviction—but not wisdom. The poem reminds believers that even our greatest insights cannot reach the depths of God's purposes. Wisdom is God's possession, not humanity's achievement.

Yet the chapter does not leave us in silence. God reveals the wisdom we most need: to fear him and to turn from evil. The call is not to understand everything but to walk faithfully when understanding fails. This is the kind of wisdom Job will need as God prepares to speak from the whirlwind. And it is the wisdom Christians must embrace in every season of confusion, grief, or unanswered prayer.

REFLECTION

1. What part of Job 28 most helps you accept the limits of your own understanding?

2. How does the poem's contrast between human achievement and human limitation challenge your assumptions about wisdom?

3. Why is it comforting to know that God alone fully understands the deep structure of creation and providence?

4. How does "the fear of the Lord" reshape the way you think about suffering and obedience?

5. Where in your life do you sense the need for moral wisdom more than explanatory answers?

6. How might accepting mystery help you walk more faithfully in difficult seasons?

DISCUSSION

1. Why does Job 28 interrupt the debate between Job and his friends, and what does that interruption teach us?

2. How do the mining images in verses 1–11 illustrate both human ability and human limits?

3. Why is it significant that neither creation nor human effort can locate true wisdom?

4. What does Job 28 reveal about the difference between God's wisdom and human attempts to explain suffering?

5. How does verse 28 ("fear God, turn from evil") redefine the search for wisdom in the book of Job?

6. How should Job 28 shape the church's approach to counseling, suffering, and unanswered questions?

7

THE MAN I USED TO BE

JOB 29–31

Objective: To see how Job's past faithfulness, present anguish, and continuing integrity reveal what true righteousness is in suffering.

INTRODUCTION

In 1911, the luxury steamship *SS Yongala* disappeared off the coast of Australia during a cyclone. For decades, the wreck remained undiscovered. The ship's sudden loss left hundreds of families reeling. One survivor's relative later wrote that what haunted her most was not the tragedy itself but the contrast between the vibrant life her cousin had lived the week before and the silence that followed. "One moment he was laughing in our kitchen," she said, "and a day later, there was nothing but questions."

Loss often creates a jarring before-and-after—the life we knew and the life we never expected. Memories of what once was can deepen the ache of what now is. But they can also reveal the depth of a person's character, purpose, and relationships.

This is the emotional terrain of Job 29–31. Job remembers the man he used to be—honored, respected, useful, surrounded by God's blessing and human gratitude. Then he names the man he has become—mocked, isolated, physically broken, and misunderstood. Finally, he declares the man he remains—a man of integrity who refuses to abandon truth even when life collapses.

These chapters form Job's final testimony before God. They show that while suffering changes circumstances, it does not have to change character—and that a life shaped by righteousness matters deeply when everything else falls away.

EXAMINATION

A final testimony before God (29:1)

Job 29–31 forms Job's closing argument—his last long speech before Elihu enters and before God speaks from the whirlwind. These chapters are not an emotional outburst but a deliberate, structured, and deeply personal testimony. Job is not defending himself before the friends anymore; he is addressing God. He longs for vindication, not victory. These chapters reveal a man looking back on the life he once lived (chapter 29), naming the life he now endures (chapter 30), and affirming the integrity he continues to maintain (chapter 31).

Taken together, they form one of the most profound self-examinations in Scripture. They show that Job's righteousness was not an illusion. His suffering did not erase his character. His grief did not silence his integrity. Job is not trying to prove perfection—only honesty. He insists that the person he once was is the same person he still is, even though circumstances have changed beyond recognition.

Remembering honor, blessing, and usefulness (29:2–20)

Job begins with a wistful longing: "Oh, that I were as in months gone by." He remembers his former life with gratitude and sorrow. The chapter is filled with images of intimacy with God—"when God watched over me," "when his lamp shone upon my head," "when the friendship of God was upon my tent." Job's memory is not nostalgic fantasy; it is the testimony of a life once marked by divine favor and nearness.

He recalls walking through the city gates and being greeted with honor. The young withdrew out of respect; the aged rose in acknowledgment. People listened when he spoke. His words carried weight because his character carried weight. Job was known for justice, generosity, and protection of the vulnerable. He rescued the poor, defended the fatherless, and comforted the dying. "I put on righteousness, and it clothed me," he says, a metaphor that captures how naturally holiness shaped his daily life.

Job's memory is not pride. It is grief over the loss of relationship, purpose, and community. Honor had flowed from a life immersed in reverence. Job is acknowledging what once was so he can contrast it with what now is.

A life unraveling—pain, mockery, and alienation (30:1–15)

Chapter 30 shifts tone abruptly. Job moves from "the man I used to be" to "the man I have become." The reversal is stark. Those who once respected him now mock him. Men whose fathers he once would not have trusted around his flocks now laugh at his misery. Job is not demeaning the poor; he is revealing how far his social position has fallen. The powerful have become powerless. The respected has become ridiculed.

Suffering has stripped him of dignity. He is "a byword," "a joke," "a target" for those who spit in his face. Job's physical torment mirrors his social torment: his skin is blackened, his bones burn, his harp has turned to mourning. The man who once brought comfort now needs comfort. The man who once was listened to now cannot get a hearing.

Job's lament here shows the relational and emotional dimensions of suffering. Pain is never just physical. It isolates, confuses, and distorts how others perceive us. Job's world has reversed—not because he changed, but because his circumstances have.

Feeling abandoned by God (30:16–23)

Job does not accuse God of injustice, but he does confess that he feels abandoned. "You have turned cruel to me," he says—a statement of perception, not accusation. Job speaks from anguish, not rebellion. He cannot reconcile his memories of divine friendship with his present sense of divine silence.

He describes God as throwing him into the wind, dissolving his prosperity, and refusing to answer his cries. Job does not deny God's power—he struggles to understand how that power meets his pain. His lament is relational: "I cry to you for help and you do not answer me." These words echo the Psalms of lament, showing that faithful believers may feel forsaken without losing their faith.

Job's fear is not death but dying without understanding God's posture toward him. He believes God will bring him to Sheol, but he wrestles with the seeming absence of mercy in the process. His questions do not deny God's existence; they arise from longing for God's presence.

Job's integrity under oath (31:1–12)

Chapter 31 forms Job's formal oath of innocence. This is not self-righteous boasting; it is covenant language. Job calls curses upon himself if he has committed any sin the friends have implied. He begins with the heart: "I have made a covenant with my eyes." Job understands that righteousness begins with small decisions in private places. He examines motives, discipline, and purity.

He denies adultery, deception, and hidden desires. If he has acted in these ways, he says, then let God judge him. Job is not claiming that he has never sinned—only that he has not lived a life that deserves this ruin. His oath reflects clarity of conscience, not arrogance.

Job's testimony reveals a truth that threads through the book: integrity is not situational; it is cultivated long before the storm arrives.

Job's social righteousness (31:13–23)

Job's righteousness extended beyond personal morality into how he treated others, especially the vulnerable. He refuses to exploit servants. He never ignored the poor. He fed widows and clothed the needy. He welcomed orphans and strangers. Job's care for the marginalized reflects deep reverence for God, for he knows God sees all.

Job's list demonstrates biblical righteousness in practice—not ritual perfection but compassionate justice. He lived a life shaped by fairness, generosity, and mercy. His suffering is therefore doubly painful: the very people he once helped now avoid or mock him. Yet his integrity stands.

This section shows why God commended Job's character from the beginning. Job's obedience was not theoretical but embodied. He demonstrated covenant character long before the friends accused him of covenant violation.

Job rejects idolatry of heart and hand (31:24–34)

Job continues his oath by denying idolatry in all its forms. He has not trusted in gold or wealth. He has not worshiped sun or moon. He has not rejoiced at the downfall of enemies. He has not hidden sin or deceived others for fear of public shame.

The list reveals how deeply Job understands the nature of temptation. Idolatry is not only bowing before a statue—it is trusting anything more than God. Job has kept his heart guarded and his motives pure.

He then recounts how he opened his home to travelers and practiced genuine hospitality. Job's righteousness is holistic—moral, social, sexual, economic, and spiritual. He lived an integrated life.

Job's closing appeal (31:35–40)

Job ends with one final cry: "Oh, that I had someone to hear me!" He desires an audience before God—someone to weigh his case, examine his life, and judge fairly. He is not asking for vindication before people but before the Almighty.

He signs his testimony with metaphorical ink, calling God to respond. He even invites curses upon his land if he is lying. These are not hollow words but the earnest plea of a man who values truth more than comfort.

Job concludes not with triumph but with trembling hope. He has said all he can say. Now he longs for God to speak. His final words do not resolve the tension—they intensify it. For the first time, Job stops talking. The courtroom is quiet. The next voice will break the silence in a way Job never expected.

APPLICATION

1. Faithfulness in the past strengthens faithfulness in the present

Job remembers a season when life was marked by God's nearness, personal usefulness, and community respect. Those memories deepen his grief, but they also reveal the strength of long-formed integrity. A life shaped by righteousness does not evaporate in crisis; it anchors believers when suffering strikes. Christians sometimes worry that hardship will unravel their faith, but Job shows the opposite: the habits of holiness built over years become the roots that hold when storms come. Your past faithfulness is not wasted. Every choice to obey, every act of kindness, and every step of integrity becomes part of the foundation that supports you when life collapses. Suffering may shake confidence, but it cannot erase a character formed by consistent reverence. The work Christians do in quiet seasons prepares them for the trials that come without warning.

2. Suffering often feels like isolation—and God invites honesty in that loneliness

Job's transition from chapter 29 to 30 is emotionally jarring. A man once honored and surrounded now feels mocked and alone. He even feels as though God has turned against him. This reveals something every believer experiences at some point: suffering isolates. It changes relationships, disrupts routines, and alters how others see us. Yet Job does something crucial—he speaks honestly to God about that isolation. He refuses to hide his confusion or mute his anguish. Christians sometimes fear that such honesty dishonors God, but Scripture teaches the opposite. Lament is not rebellion; it is relationship. When you feel abandoned or unseen, God invites you to bring that loneliness into his presence. Job's example shows that God is not threatened by sorrow spoken in faith.

3. Integrity is forged long before it is tested

Chapter 31 reveals the depth of Job's character. His righteousness was not a performance for people; it was a covenant with God. He guarded his eyes, his motives, his actions, and his relationships long before anyone saw the fruit of that discipline. When suffering came, he did not crumble because his integrity was not situational. Many Christians hope to stand strong in trial without investing in holiness in ordinary moments. Job teaches that strength under pressure is built through daily commitments—small decisions, quiet obedience, and private discipline. Christians cannot expect integrity to emerge suddenly in crisis if it has not been nurtured slowly over time. A life shaped by righteousness does not guarantee ease, but it equips believers to endure hardship without compromising their commitment to God.

4. God values truth in the inward being

Job ends his speech with a daring declaration: he invites God to examine him fully. This is not arrogance but confidence in the God who sees plainly. Job's greatest concern is not escape from suffering but alignment with truth. His willingness to open his heart before God challenges believers to pursue authenticity in both thought and action. Christians sometimes feel pressure to appear spiritually composed even when struggling, but God is not impressed by appearances. He values honesty, repentance, humility, and integrity. When Christians lay their lives openly before the Lord, they demonstrate trust in his mercy and love. Job's posture encourages us to live with transparency, asking God to shape us, correct us, and confirm righteousness within us. A heart open to God's examination is a heart ready for transformation.

CONCLUSION

Job 29–31 brings together the full weight of Job's story. He remembers the life he once lived, filled with God's friendship, public respect, and purposeful service. He names the life he now endures, marked by mockery, isolation, and physical agony. And he affirms the life he continues to uphold—a life of integrity shaped long before suffering came. These chapters do not answer Job's questions, but they do reveal his heart.

Job's final testimony shows that righteousness is not proven by circumstances but by character. The man who once walked in blessing now walks through pain, yet he remains faithful. His memories deepen his longing, his suffering sharpens his honesty, and his integrity prepares him for the moment when God will finally speak. Job stands before God not demanding reward but asking for truth. His closing words invite believers to do the same—trusting that a life formed by reverence endures even when everything else falls apart.

REFLECTION

1. What emotions surface in you as you read Job's contrast between his former honor and his present suffering?

2. How does Job's honest expression of feeling abandoned by God help shape your understanding of faithful lament?

3. In what ways do Job's memories of past closeness with God deepen, rather than diminish, his present faith?

4. Which parts of Job's integrity in chapter 31 challenge you to examine your own private commitments before God?

5. How does Job's willingness to let God "weigh him" encourage you to pursue deeper honesty in your spiritual life?

6. Where do you most need to trust that long-formed faithfulness still matters, even in seasons of confusion?

DISCUSSION

1. Why do you think Job spends so much time remembering his former life in chapter 29?

2. How does chapter 30 reveal the relational and emotional dimensions of suffering that theological explanations often miss?

3. What makes Job's oath in chapter 31 different from self-righteous boasting? What does it reveal about his character?

4. How does the structure of these chapters (past → present → integrity) strengthen Job's final appeal to God?

5. Why is it important for churches to make space for Christians to express feelings of abandonment, confusion, or grief?

6. How can Job 29–31 help Christians understand that righteousness does not guarantee ease but does sustain endurance?

8

THE VOICE OF THE YOUNGER MAN
JOB 32-37

Objective: To understand how Elihu reframes suffering and prepares Job to hear God by emphasizing divine wisdom, justice, and care.

INTRODUCTION

In 1986, during preparations for NASA's Voyager 2 encounter with Uranus, engineers were struggling to interpret unexpected data from one of the spacecraft's instruments. Senior specialists debated possible malfunctions, each confident in his explanation. In the middle of the discussion, an intern—Lisa Hardaway, then a young aerospace student—quietly pointed out an overlooked calibration issue involving temperature fluctuations on the spacecraft.

Her observation was simple, but it reframed the entire problem. The team reanalyzed the data using her suggestion, and the issue was resolved. Later, senior engineers acknowledged that her insight prevented a costly misdiagnosis of the spacecraft's condition. One scientist remarked, "Wisdom sometimes comes from the person no one expects to speak."

Elihu plays that role in Job 32-37. He is younger, less authoritative, and has waited respectfully for the older men to speak. Yet when he finally steps forward, he offers what no one else has: a perspective that is both theologically rich and pastorally balanced. He does not accuse Job of hidden sin, nor does he dismiss Job's anguish. Instead, he insists that suffering may be formative rather than punitive, and that God's greatness does not negate his compassion.

Elihu's voice does not compete with God's—it prepares the way for God's. Before the whirlwind speaks, a younger man helps Job lift his eyes.

EXAMINATION

Why Elihu speaks (32:1–5)

After Job's final appeal in chapters 29–31, a silence settles over the scene. The three friends have nothing left to say. Their arguments are exhausted, their theology exposed, and their certainty drained. Into that quiet steps a younger man—Elihu, son of Barachel. His appearance surprises readers because he has been present all along but silent out of respect for his elders. Now, seeing that the friends cannot answer Job and that Job continues to defend his righteousness without resolution, Elihu's anger "burns" within him.

His anger is not petty frustration but relational and theological concern. He believes the friends have failed because they condemned Job without proving anything. He believes Job has failed because his desire for vindication risks implying that God has acted unjustly. So Elihu speaks—not to condemn or to defend a rigid system, but to redirect the entire conversation. He is not God's judge, nor Job's prosecutor. He believes he is a mediator who can help both sides see truth more clearly.

Elihu is a complex figure—neither villain nor hero. His speeches contain insight and presumption, truth and excess. But he offers something the friends never did: fresh categories through which to think about suffering.

Elihu's method: Humility with conviction (32:6–22)

Elihu begins by acknowledging his youth. He does not assume wisdom based on age or position but claims wisdom rooted in the "spirit in man" and "the breath of the Almighty." His humility is genuine, though not flawless. He refuses flattery and vows to speak honestly before God. He insists that wisdom is not the property of the aged alone.

His approach differs from the friends in two important ways: (1) He does not accuse Job of secret sin. (2) He emphasizes God's character rather than Job's failures. Elihu believes Job has gone too far in justifying himself, but he does not assume Job's suffering must be punishment. This distinction prepares the reader for God's speeches, where the focus shifts from Job's righteousness to God's greatness. Elihu becomes a bridge between human debate and divine declaration.

Suffering as instruction, not accusation (33:1-18)

Elihu's first major insight is that God uses suffering to speak—not to condemn, but to instruct. He rejects the idea that pain is always punitive. Instead, he presents suffering as a means by which God warns, refines, humbles, and saves.

He describes God speaking in dreams, visions, and affliction to turn a person "from the pit." This is the first time in the book someone suggests that suffering may serve a corrective or protective purpose without implying moral guilt. Elihu broadens the theology of suffering beyond the friends' narrow retribution model.

This does not mean Elihu explains Job's suffering fully. But he introduces a more nuanced framework: God may allow suffering not because someone is wicked, but because God is shaping something deeper that cannot be accomplished through prosperity.

A theology of redemption in suffering (33:19-33)

Elihu adds another layer: God sometimes uses affliction to rescue. He presents suffering as a severe mercy that draws the afflicted person toward dependence and righteousness. God's purposes, he insists, are not to destroy but to deliver.

He describes God sending a "messenger" or mediator to announce deliverance and restore a person's life. This language anticipates Job's own longing for a heavenly witness. Elihu suggests that even in pain, God is at work to redeem, not simply to repay.

Although Elihu never claims Job's suffering has this specific purpose, he opens Job's imagination to the possibility that pain does not equal rejection. This turns the theological argument away from accusation and toward hope.

Elihu's defense of God's justice (34:1-37)

In his second speech, Elihu addresses Job's claim that God has treated him unjustly. Elihu does not accuse Job of rebellion; he argues that Job's words unintentionally imply that God acts without fairness. Elihu insists that God cannot do wrong and does not pervert justice.

His tone is firm, but his theology is sound. God's justice does not depend on human understanding. His sovereignty is not subject to human evaluation. Elihu reminds Job that God sees all behavior, judges impartially, and rules the world with perfect righteousness.

Though Elihu presses Job strongly, his primary goal is to lift Job's eyes from his own pain to the character of God. The friends focused on Job's guilt. Elihu focuses on God's goodness.

God does not owe explanations (35:1-16)

Elihu's third speech speaks directly to Job's frustration with divine silence. He tells Job that human righteousness or wickedness does not enrich or diminish God. God is not obligated to respond on human terms.

This is not dismissal—it is perspective. Elihu gently reminds Job that God's transcendence means he acts according to his will, not human demands. Suffering does not obligate God to provide immediate answers.

Elihu also critiques empty cries for help—those rooted not in genuine repentance or trust, but in frustration or entitlement. This pushes Job to consider the posture of his heart, not simply the content of his complaints.

A God who is great, powerful, and yet attentive (36:1-23)

Elihu's final speeches are theologically rich. He proclaims God's greatness, power, and wisdom, but unlike the friends, he pairs this with compassion. God watches over his people, exalts the humble, and teaches through trials. Elihu portrays God as both majestic and merciful.

He insists that God uses suffering to "open the ears" of the afflicted—to draw them toward maturity and righteousness. Again, Elihu does not say Job sinned. Instead, he argues that suffering can be formative even when not deserved.

Elihu believes that if Job listens, he may find that God is using this season not to punish but to refine and deepen his understanding.

A summons to behold God's work (36:24-37:24)

Elihu concludes by pointing Job toward God's majesty in creation. Thunder, lightning, snow, rain, and storm all testify to divine power and wisdom. In these chapters, Elihu becomes the narrator who prepares Job for the whirlwind.

His message is simple: "Job, you cannot understand everything God does, but you can trust the One who governs creation."

Elihu's speech shifts the focus from Job's experience to God's character. This movement anticipates exactly what God will do in chapters 38–41. Elihu's voice is not a replacement for God's voice, but a preparation for it. He tells Job to stand still, consider God's works, and recognize that the Creator's wisdom surpasses human comprehension.

Elihu ends by calling Job to reverence. He does not declare Job a sinner; he declares God supreme. His speeches acknowledge Job's pain while insisting that God's greatness and goodness are not diminished by that pain. In doing so, Elihu provides the theological bridge between human wrestling and divine revelation.

APPLICATION

1. God may use suffering to shape us, not punish us

Elihu's greatest contribution is his insistence that suffering is not always a sign of divine anger. Sometimes God uses difficulty to humble the proud, protect the vulnerable, or draw the faithful into deeper dependence. This does not mean every hardship serves a clear corrective purpose, nor does it mean believers should assume guilt when life hurts. Instead, Elihu invites us to consider that God may be working in ways we cannot yet see. Pain becomes a tool in God's hands—not to destroy, but to refine. Christians today often look for quick explanations, but God's purposes are rarely simple. Suffering may reveal sin, but it may also deepen faith, sharpen character, or redirect our hearts toward eternal things. Elihu reminds believers that God's hand can be present in affliction even when his reasons remain hidden.

2. God's greatness does not diminish his care

Elihu emphasizes God's sovereignty—his power over creation, his rule over nations, his control over storms and seasons. Yet he also insists that God watches the righteous, hears the humble, and acts with justice. This pairing of transcendence and attentiveness is essential. Christians sometimes imagine that God is either too majestic to notice their struggles or too busy to care. Elihu corrects this by showing that God's greatness is the foundation of his care. Because God is sovereign, he is never overwhelmed. Because he is just, he never overlooks those who suffer. Suffering does not place a believer outside God's concern; it places them squarely within his compassionate attention. Elihu calls us to trust not only in God's power but in his goodness.

3. Humility prepares the heart to hear God

Elihu confronts both Job and the friends with the same truth: human wisdom has limits. Job's friends spoke with certainty but lacked compassion. Job spoke with honesty but sometimes lost perspective. Elihu understands that wisdom begins with humility—the recognition that God does not owe us explanations and that our understanding cannot grasp the depths of his purposes. When believers demand answers, they often close themselves off to the deeper work God may be doing. But humility opens the heart to correction, guidance, and renewed perspective. Elihu's call is not to silence our questions, but to bring them to God with reverence. Humility does not solve suffering, but it prepares believers to hear God when he speaks.

4. God's silence is not absence

Elihu addresses the very tension that torments Job: why does God seem silent? Elihu does not deny the silence, but he reframes it. God may delay answers not out of neglect, but because he aims to reshape the heart, reveal hidden assumptions, or deepen trust. Divine silence can be a season of preparation—an invitation to wait, listen, and remember God's character. Christians often equate silence with abandonment, but Elihu insists otherwise. God remains present, even when he withholds immediate clarity. His silence is not emptiness; it is an opportunity to strengthen faith and cultivate patience. When Christians endure seasons where God feels distant, Elihu encourages them to keep seeking, keep praying, and keep trusting. God's voice may not come when we expect, but it always comes at the right time.

CONCLUSION

Elihu's speeches stand as a turning point in the book of Job. He does not fall into the harsh accusations of the three friends, nor does he accept Job's assumption that God has acted unjustly. Instead, he invites Job to see suffering from a broader, more hopeful perspective. God may use affliction not merely to correct but to instruct, refine, and rescue. Elihu's theology acknowledges mystery without denying God's goodness.

He also restores reverence to the conversation. By directing Job's attention to the majesty of creation and the character of God, Elihu prepares the way for the voice from the whirlwind. Job will not receive explanations—he will receive revelation. And Elihu's final call to behold God's works helps Job approach that moment with humility rather than accusation.

These chapters teach believers that when answers fail, reverence remains. Elihu reminds us that God is great in power and rich in mercy, and that the wisest posture in suffering is not certainty, but trust.

REFLECTION

1. How does Elihu's perspective on suffering challenge or encourage you compared to the friends' speeches?

2. Where have you seen God use hardship in your own life to shape faith or redirect your steps?

3. What parts of Elihu's description of God's greatness bring you the most comfort in seasons of uncertainty?

4. How does Elihu's call to humility change the way you process unanswered questions?

5. Why is it important to recognize that God's silence does not equal his absence?

6. Which part of Elihu's teaching helps you trust God more deeply when life feels confusing?

DISCUSSION

1. Why does Elihu wait until the older men have finished speaking before offering his perspective?

2. What makes Elihu's approach to suffering different from the retribution theology of Job's three friends?

3. How does Elihu broaden Job's understanding of how God might use suffering in a believer's life?

4. Why is Elihu's emphasis on God's greatness essential preparation for God's speeches in chapters 38–41?

5. How does Elihu help correct both Job's frustration and the friends' accusations?

6. What practical lessons can the church learn from Elihu about how to speak to others who are suffering?

9

GOD SPEAKS

JOB 38:1–40:2

Objective: To see how God's revelation of his power in creation reshapes our understanding of suffering and restores reverence.

INTRODUCTION

In 1968, during the historic Apollo 8 mission, astronauts Frank Borman, Jim Lovell, and Bill Anders became the first humans to orbit the moon. As their spacecraft emerged from the dark side on Christmas Eve, Anders captured the now-famous "Earthrise" photograph—the earth rising above the lunar horizon, a small blue sphere suspended in blackness.

The astronauts later described the moment as overwhelming. They had traveled nearly a quarter-million miles to explore another world, but the sight that stunned them most was their own planet—fragile, beautiful, and impossibly small. Borman said, "We came all this way to explore the moon, and the most important thing we discovered was the Earth."

The moment reoriented their perspective. The boundaries and struggles that felt enormous from the surface shrank against the backdrop of cosmic grandeur. Problems were not solved, but the scale had changed—and with it, their sense of awe.

That is what happens in Job 38–40. When God speaks from the whirlwind, he does not enter Job's courtroom or offer a detailed explanation for

Job's pain. Instead, he lifts Job's eyes to creation—its foundations, its weather patterns, its constellations, its untamed animals. God does not minimize Job's suffering; he magnifies his own majesty.

Job had demanded answers; God gives him a new horizon. Divine wisdom, woven into the cosmos, becomes the lens through which Job must relearn trust. Before Job's circumstances change, his perspective must.

EXAMINATION

The God who answers from the whirlwind (38:1–3)

Job has pleaded for an audience with God since chapter 13. He has cried for a mediator, longed for vindication, and begged for clarity. He wanted God to step into the courtroom so he could present his case. Yet when God finally answers, he does not come as a silent judge seated behind a bench. He comes in a whirlwind—majestic, overwhelming, uncontainable.

The whirlwind is not punishment but revelation. Throughout Scripture, storms accompany theophanies: God appears in thunder at Sinai, rides on the storm in the Psalms, and speaks through tempest and cloud. When God arrives in Job 38, he does not crush Job; he summons him. "Dress for action like a man." God invites Job into dialogue, but on God's terms, not Job's.

This opening reveals something essential: God takes Job's suffering seriously. God does not ignore him. Divine silence ends with divine presence. But God does not begin with explanations or comfort—he begins with questions designed to expand Job's vision far beyond the boundaries of his grief.

Job wanted an answer to his pain; God gives him a revelation of his power. Job wanted reasons; God gives perspective. God is not avoiding Job's concerns—he is addressing them at their foundation. Before Job can understand suffering, he must understand the God who governs the world.

Creation as God's first answer to human pain (38:4–21)

God's first question cuts deeply: "Where were you when I laid the foundation of the earth?" Job has spent chapters asking how God governs the world. God responds by examining the world Job wants him to explain.

God's questions are poetic, not sarcastic. He is not belittling Job; he is inviting Job into wonder. Job has argued as though the world is morally simple.

The friends have insisted that justice is immediate and predictable. But God points to creation and says, in effect: "You cannot judge what you cannot see."

The imagery is expansive: foundations laid, measurements set, the cornerstone placed while "the morning stars sang together." This is not a lecture in cosmology but a vision of divine craftsmanship. The world is not chaos; it is structure. The universe is not arbitrary; it is designed. Job's suffering feels like disorder, but the cosmos is anything but disordered.

God continues with images of the sea bursting from the womb, swaddled in clouds, contained by boundaries. These pictures are tender and powerful—God as midwife, architect, and warrior. He asks Job if he has commanded the dawn or walked the recesses of the deep. These realms are beyond Job's knowledge, yet they are familiar terrain to God.

The message is clear: "Job, you see only a fragment. I see the whole."

The world's hidden structures and sovereign boundaries (38:22–38)

The next series of questions moves from cosmic origins to the operations of the natural world. Snow, hail, lightning, rain, ice, stars, clouds, and the rhythms of nature—all operate under God's direction. What Job experiences as randomness, God governs with precision.

The friends believed they understood how justice works because they had observed patterns. Job believed God must explain himself because Job's experience broke those patterns. God reveals that both perspectives are too small.

Humans can predict weather, but they cannot speak to storm clouds and command rain. Humans can name constellations, but they cannot loosen Orion's belt or lead the Bear with her children. Humans can observe nature but cannot orchestrate it.

Job cannot govern the physical world or the moral world. God alone can. The divine interrogation is not to silence Job's lament but to reorient his assumptions. Job suffers because he cannot see the whole tapestry; God sees every thread.

This portion of the speech shows that creation is not a simple, predictable machine. It is a living, dynamic system built with freedom and complexity. If the physical world is so intricate that Job cannot master it, how could Job presume to master the moral order that governs suffering?

God's wild and wondrous creatures (38:39–39:30)

After surveying the foundations and forces of creation, God turns Job's attention to living creatures. These animals are wild, untamed, and free—creatures that do not fit easily into human categories or control.

This turn in the divine speech is deliberate. Humans often prefer systems they can manage, explanations they can master, and moral formulas they can predict. The friends' theology demanded a world that worked like a farm: sow righteousness, reap blessing; sow wickedness, reap disaster.

But the animal kingdom refuses such simplicity.

- Lions rely on God, not people, for provision.
- Ravens cry to God, not humans, for food.
- Mountain goats give birth in hidden places under God's watchful eye.
- The wild donkey runs free where humans cannot direct it.
- The wild ox is powerful but cannot be domesticated.
- The ostrich is foolish but fast—a paradox built into its nature.
- The horse snorts with fierce courage, charging into battle without fear.
- The hawk and eagle soar by God's instinctive direction, commanding the skies from their heights.

God's point is profound: the world is full of creatures that thrive outside human management. Their existence reveals a God who delights in wildness, freedom, and beauty. If creation itself is richer, wilder, and more complex than humans can grasp, how much more is God's providence?

This is the answer Job needed, though not the one he expected. God's world is not a tight, mechanistic system; it is an expansive, dynamic universe governed by divine wisdom.

Job's problem was not doubt but perspective (40:1)

God pauses briefly: "Shall a faultfinder contend with the Almighty?" God is not attacking Job's character—he is exposing the limits of Job's vantage point. Job believed that if God would only answer, the mystery of his suffering would be solved. God reveals that the real issue is not the lack of explanation but the lack of perspective.

Job's cries came from anguish, not arrogance. But anguish can still narrow vision. God's creation speech expands Job's view so he can see his suffering not as a referendum on justice but as part of a world too vast for easy categorization.

God is not saying Job is wrong to lament. He is saying Job is wrong to assume he has the categories to evaluate God's governance.

Creation language as divine correction (40:2)

God's questions do more than humble Job—they correct the theological assumptions of the entire debate.

- To Job: "You are not abandoned; you are limited. Trust the God who holds the world you cannot see."
- To the friends: "You thought you understood justice, but you misunderstood the universe."
- To all readers: "Do not judge God's ways by your limited field of vision."

God's creation speech restores order not by solving Job's riddle but by revealing the greatness of the Creator. When God speaks of creation, he is not avoiding the problem of suffering; he is addressing it at the deepest level possible. Suffering is too complex for simple answers, but not too deep for the God who laid the foundations of the earth.

APPLICATION

1. Let God's greatness reshape your understanding of suffering

When God finally speaks, he does not explain Job's suffering—he reveals his power, wisdom, and care in creation. This teaches believers that understanding suffering begins not with reasons but with reverence. We often assume that pain requires explanation, but God invites us to see suffering through the lens of who he is rather than what we feel. His majesty reveals that our perspective is limited and that his purposes extend far beyond what we perceive. When hardship strikes, the most faithful response is not to demand answers but to turn our eyes toward the God who laid the foundations of the earth. His greatness does not diminish our pain; it places our pain within a world governed by infinite wisdom. We learn to trust not because we understand, but because we know the One who does.

2. God's world is larger than our expectations

Job and his friends wanted a predictable universe—a world where righteous behavior guarantees blessing and sin guarantees suffering. But God's creation speech shows that the world is far more complex and wondrous than human systems allow. The animal kingdom, unpredictable weather patterns, and the vastness of creation reveal that God delights in freedom, beauty, and mystery. Christians often struggle when life does not fit into neat categories or expected patterns. Yet Job 38–40 reminds us that God's governance is not constrained by our assumptions. Instead of forcing life into simple formulas, Christians are called to embrace the vastness of God's world and trust that he reigns over it with perfect wisdom. Accepting mystery is not weakness—it is a form of worship.

3. God's presence is more healing than God's explanations

Job longed for God to speak. When God finally does, he offers no explanation for Job's suffering—only himself. This reveals a profound truth: divine presence sustains the believer more deeply than divine answers ever could. Explanations may satisfy curiosity, but presence heals the soul. Many Christians imagine that peace will come when they understand "why" something happened, but God shows Job that peace comes from encountering the God who holds all things together. In seasons when God seems silent, we assume he is absent, yet Scripture teaches that silence does not negate presence. When God reveals himself, Job's anxiety begins to melt—not because his questions are solved, but because his heart has seen the One who reigns. The greatest comfort in suffering is not information but communion.

4. Humility is the gateway to restored faith

God's questions were not designed to shame Job but to humble him. Humility is not humiliation—it is clarity. It is recognizing the gap between the Creator and the creature. When believers confront suffering with humility, they remember that their perspective is limited and that God's perspective is limitless. Humility does not silence lament; it guides lament. It acknowledges that while the world feels chaotic, God remains wise, powerful, and attentive. Job's restoration begins not when his fortunes change but when his vision changes. By embracing humility, Christians open themselves to deeper trust and renewed reverence. God's world is vaster than our comprehension, and humility helps us surrender the need for control and rest in the One who commands the morning, feeds the ravens, and calls the stars by name.

CONCLUSION

When God finally answers Job, the conversation does not move toward explanation but toward revelation. God's questions lift Job's eyes from the ash heap to the architecture of the universe—from his broken body to the vast, wild, ordered world God sustains each moment. Job's suffering has not been dismissed; it has been reoriented beneath the weight of divine majesty.

These chapters teach believers that faith is not strengthened by having all the answers but by beholding the God who holds all things together. The Creator who commands the morning, feeds the ravens, watches over mountain goats, and sends lightning across the sky is the same God who hears the cries of the righteous sufferer. God's greatness does not diminish his care—it magnifies it.

Before Job's fortunes change, his sight changes. He discovers that the God who governs creation can be trusted even when life makes no sense. And that vision prepares him for the next movement in the book—the One who will challenge him further and lead him into deeper humility.

REFLECTION

1. What part of God's creation speech most reshapes how you think about your own suffering?

2. How does the imagery of the whirlwind affect your understanding of God's presence in pain?

3. Where do you see your own expectations of how life "should work" challenged by Job 38–40?

4. Why do you think God chose to speak about creation instead of giving Job explanations?

5. How does God's focus on wild and untamed creatures affect the way you view God's wisdom?

6. In what area of your life do you most need humility before God's majesty?

DISCUSSION

1. Why is it significant that God answers Job directly after so many chapters of silence?

2. How do God's questions about the foundations of the earth expose the limits of human understanding?

3. Why does God point to the natural world—weather, stars, animals—when responding to Job's complaints about justice?

4. How does the creation speech correct both Job's assumptions and the friends' rigid theology?

5. In what ways does this passage teach that God's presence is more important than explanations?

6. How can Christians cultivate a deeper reverence for God when facing seasons of confusion or pain?

10

GOD SPEAKS AGAIN

JOB 40:3-41:38

Objective: To learn how God's revelation of Behemoth and Leviathan enlarges our perspective and invites deeper trust in his sovereign wisdom.

INTRODUCTION

In 1859, a young naturalist named Alfred Russel Wallace was exploring the rainforests of Borneo when he encountered a creature he had only heard described in stories: the giant reticulated python. Wallace later wrote that nothing prepared him for the sight of an animal so powerful, so silent, and so strangely majestic. Local hunters told him that a full-grown python could drag down a deer, vanish into the river, and disappear without a trace.

Wallace was an experienced explorer—he had cataloged insects, survived tropical fevers, and mapped unknown terrain. But before this creature he felt something unexpected: awe. The python did not threaten him directly, yet he realized it existed beyond the reach of human control. The forest belonged to it far more than it belonged to any human.

Wallace's journals reveal that the encounter reshaped his view of the natural world. He had spent years studying nature, but this moment reminded him that creation contains forces and creatures humans cannot domesticate, predict, or master. Such encounters do not diminish our place in the world—they deepen our reverence for its Maker.

That is precisely what happens in Job 40–41. God directs Job's attention to Behemoth and Leviathan—not to frighten him, but to expand his understanding. Job has wrestled with suffering he cannot control and mysteries he cannot solve. Instead of offering explanations, God reveals creatures whose very existence testifies to divine wisdom and power far beyond human reach. Through these magnificent beings, God teaches Job that trust does not come from mastering the world, but from beholding the One who does.

EXAMINATION

Job's humbled silence and God's continued invitation (40:3–5)

After God's first whirlwind speech, Job is no longer defiant. He places his hand over his mouth, overwhelmed not by shame but by awe. He realizes he has spoken beyond his limits. Yet God does not send him away. Instead, God continues speaking—not because Job failed to understand the first speech, but because Job is now ready to hear more. What comes next is not rebuke but revelation, a deepening of the vision God began to give in chapters 38–39. Job's humility opens a door, and God steps through it, inviting him to see the world with clearer eyes and a larger heart.

Why God speaks of creatures instead of causes

It may seem strange that God's answer to a suffering man focuses not on moral arguments or heavenly mysteries, but on two enormous creatures. But God's goal is not to answer Job's questions one by one; it is to restore Job's vision. Job's pain had narrowed his world until all he could see was injustice. God widens that world again. Behemoth and Leviathan are not distractions—they are windows into a universe Job had forgotten. Through them, God teaches Job that the world is bigger, stranger, more wondrous, and more ordered than Job imagined. Explanations would have addressed Job's mind; these creatures address his heart.

Behemoth: Embodiment of God's ordered strength (40:6–24)

God first directs Job's attention to Behemoth, a creature as real as any animal Job knew, yet described with such grandeur that it stands as a living symbol of power beyond human command. Its bones are like bronze, its limbs like iron. It feeds peacefully on grass, yet its sheer size makes it untouchable. Floodwaters surge around it, but it remains unshaken. No hunter can subdue it, no human can harness it. Behemoth is part of God's world, not ours—a glimpse into a creation that includes creatures strong, free, and utterly beyond human control.

The point is not to identify Behemoth with precision but to see what God sees: a creature whose existence reveals both the magnificence and the mystery of divine craftsmanship. If Job cannot master Behemoth, how can he assume he understands the workings of providence? If Job cannot govern the physical world, how could he hope to judge the moral one? Behemoth stands before Job as a gentle but firm reminder that God oversees a world whose depths Job cannot plumb.

Leviathan: Face of untamable wildness (41:1–34)

If Behemoth represents strength, Leviathan represents terror. God's description of Leviathan stretches the animal beyond its normal proportions, portraying it in language that captures the awe it inspired in ancient readers. Smoke pours from its nostrils, fire flashes from its mouth, and its scales form an impenetrable shield. Warriors retreat in fear; harpoons and swords bounce off its body. The sea churns white behind it as it moves. Whether rooted in the crocodile or another massive sea creature, Leviathan is depicted as the embodiment of nature's wildest, most uncontrollable power.

Yet Leviathan is not God's enemy. God delights in describing it. The creature that terrifies humanity is, to God, simply another marvelous work of his hands. This is the heart of the lesson: *if Job fears what God controls effortlessly, then Job's fear can give way to trust.* Leviathan's uncontrollable strength mirrors the overwhelming forces that swept through Job's life. But while Job could not tame those forces, God holds complete mastery over them.

What these creatures reveal about God's world

The descriptions of Behemoth and Leviathan are not zoological puzzles for readers to solve; they are theological portraits. Together, they show a world that contains both order and wildness. God has filled his creation with creatures that obey no human command and fit no human category. Yet these same creatures exist within boundaries God himself established.

Job's mistake was not his honesty—God never rebukes him for lament. Job's mistake was assuming the world should work according to human-scale simplicity. The friends shared the same error in reverse: they assumed that if the world is predictable, then Job must have sinned. God corrects both views by revealing a world that is both structured and mysterious, magnificent and untamable, rooted in God's wisdom yet far beyond human reach.

Behemoth and Leviathan remind Job that God is not a small deity who governs by rigid formulas. He is the creator of wonders Job has never imagined. The universe is not fragile or chaotic; it is vast and God-ruled—even in its wildest corners.

The rhetorical force of God's challenge (40:1–2; 41:10–11)

God asks Job whether he can confront these creatures or command them. The answer is clear. But the questions do not humiliate—they liberate. Job no longer bears the weight of deciphering the universe. He no longer carries the burden of judging God's actions. If Job cannot subdue Behemoth, he is not expected to subdue the complexities of his own suffering. If Leviathan is terrifying to humans but tame to God, then the forces that overwhelmed Job never lay outside God's care.

God's climactic statement—"Everything under heaven is mine"—is not a declaration of raw power but of reassuring sovereignty. A world that contains Behemoth and Leviathan is still fully under God's authority. Job may feel crushed by chaos, but God sees no chaos at all.

From explanation to encounter

The friends tried to explain Job's suffering. Job demanded that God explain it too. But God chooses a different path. He does not justify his ways; he reveals his glory. He does not correct Job's theology as much as he expands it. God's speeches shift Job from argument to astonishment, from demanding answers to beholding the One who sustains everything that exists.

Through Behemoth and Leviathan, God shows Job that a God mighty enough to create such creatures is mighty enough to govern Job's life. Divine power does not eliminate mystery—but it makes trust possible. Job learns not *why* he suffers, but *who* remains sovereign in his suffering. That revelation is enough to begin the healing his heart needs.

APPLICATION

1. God's sovereignty is bigger than our suffering

When God reveals Behemoth and Leviathan, he is not changing the subject—he is expanding Job's world. Job's pain felt like the center of everything, but God shows him a universe so vast and powerful that no human can grasp its boundaries. This does not minimize suffering; it places suffering inside a world governed by the God who formed creatures Job could never hope to tame. Christians often assume trust will grow once God explains our pain, but Scripture teaches that trust grows when we remember who God is. The God who masters forces far beyond human control is fully able to sustain us through seasons we do not understand. Our suffering is real, but it is not sovereign. God is. And that truth becomes an anchor when circumstances feel overwhelming.

2. Some parts of God's world are intentionally beyond our control

Behemoth and Leviathan remind Christians that God built a world containing both order and wildness. There are aspects of life we can plan, shape, and steward—and there are aspects we cannot. Modern believers often struggle with the idea that not everything can be managed or prevented. But God's creation speech teaches us that limits are not failures; they are invitations to trust. When we encounter situations we cannot fix, forces we cannot stop, or questions we cannot answer, we are facing our creaturely boundaries. Rather than producing despair, these limits can lead us to worship. They remind us that we are not God—and that it is good we are not. Recognizing this frees us from the impossible burden of running the world and helps us rest in the hands of the One who does.

3. Faith is sustained by beholding God, not by mastering explanations

Job wanted answers, and believers today often feel the same. We imagine that peace will come once we understand the reasons behind our suffering. But Job teaches that peace comes from encounter, not explanation. When God speaks, he does not offer theories; he offers himself. He draws Job's attention away from the ashes and toward the God who commands the morning, shapes the mountains, feeds the ravens, and governs the great beasts. Christians do not need to decode every mystery in life in order to walk faithfully. Instead, we grow in endurance by fixing our eyes on the God who reigns over mysteries too deep for us to solve. Explanations may calm the mind for a moment, but only God's presence calms the soul.

4. Trust grows when we accept our limits and rest in God's strength

Job's problem was never rebellion; it was perspective. He assumed that if God would simply speak, he could understand the world well enough to judge it. God shows him that trust begins when we release the illusion that we can know or control everything. Humility is not defeat—it is wisdom. It frees believers to live by reverence rather than analysis. Leviathan in particular reminds us that some forces are simply beyond human ability. Yet nothing is beyond God's reach. Christians learn to trust not by solving every difficulty, but by leaning fully on the God who governs both the ordered and the wild. Surrendering control is not the end of faith—it is the pathway into deeper reverence and stronger hope.

CONCLUSION

In God's second whirlwind speech, Job discovers that the world is far larger and more wondrous than he imagined. Behemoth and Leviathan stand before him as living testimonies to the greatness, creativity, and sovereignty of the God he serves. These creatures are not problems to solve—they are reminders that God governs forces Job cannot comprehend.

Job's suffering had narrowed his vision, drawing all his attention to his pain and to questions about justice he could not answer. God restores that vision by lifting Job's eyes to the grandeur of creation. What Job needed was not an explanation of his suffering but an encounter with the God who rules both the ordered and the untamable elements of his world.

Through Behemoth and Leviathan, Job learns that trust begins where human understanding ends. The God who delights in creatures beyond human control is more than capable of sustaining the righteous sufferer. Before restoration comes, reverence must return. God has spoken, and Job's heart is finally ready to listen.

REFLECTION

1. Where do you most identify with Job's desire for explanations rather than revelation?

2. How does seeing God delight in creatures beyond human control reshape your understanding of his sovereignty?

3. Which creature—Behemoth or Leviathan—helps you most appreciate the vastness of God's power?

4. How do these chapters challenge your assumptions about what God "should" explain or reveal?

5. What situations in your life feel like Leviathan—overwhelming, untamable, or frightening? How does God's speech speak into that?

6. Where do you sense God inviting you to release control and rest in his strength?

DISCUSSION

1. Why might God choose to speak about creation rather than provide reasons for Job's suffering?

2. How do Behemoth and Leviathan illustrate the limits of human control and the expansiveness of God's governance?

3. In what ways does the second divine speech correct both Job's assumptions and the friends' rigid theology?

4. How can God's mastery over wild, uncontrollable forces encourage believers facing personal chaos?

5. How does this passage teach that humility and trust—not explanation— are the foundations of faithful endurance?

6. What can the church learn from God's response about how to walk with those who suffer?

11

JOB'S REPENTANCE

JOB 42:1-6

Objective: To see how Job's encounter with God leads him to repent of presumption and embrace humble trust.

INTRODUCTION

In 1952, Florence Chadwick attempted to swim the twenty-six miles between Catalina Island and the California coast. Thick fog rolled in shortly after she began. For over fifteen hours she swam without seeing anything—not the shoreline, not the horizon, not even the escort boats beside her. Exhausted and discouraged, she eventually asked to be pulled from the water.

When she was lifted into the boat, Chadwick discovered she had been less than a mile from the shore. Later, she explained, "I'm not excusing myself, but if I could have seen the land, I might have made it."

Her struggle wasn't physical ability; it was visibility. The fog hid the horizon, and without sight, her strength collapsed. Two months later she tried again. The same fog appeared, but this time she reached the coast. When asked what changed, she said, "I kept the land in my mind."

Job's journey reaches a similar turning point in Job 42:1-6. His circumstances haven't changed. His wounds remain. His losses remain. But the fog has lifted—not by explanation, but by revelation. Job has not reached the end of his suffering, but he has seen the God who rules over all things. And that vision changes everything. He no longer needs the answers he once demanded; he now trusts the One he has truly seen.

EXAMINATION

Job finally speaks *to* God, not *about* God (42:1–2)

Up to this point in the book, Job has spoken often and passionately—but rarely to God. He has prayed, pleaded, protested, and lamented, but his speeches have mostly been directed toward the friends or toward the idea of God rather than God himself. The whirlwind changes this. God's voice has broken the silence, and now Job answers the Lord directly. This is the first true conversation between the two.

Job begins not with apology but with confession of truth: "I know that you can do all things, and that no purpose of yours can be thwarted." He acknowledges God's sovereignty, power, and unshakable purpose. This is not a new doctrine for Job; he has always believed these things. But now he speaks them with fresh humility, having seen God's majesty rather than merely hearing about it. God's speeches have not crushed Job; they have clarified God's greatness and Job's place within that greatness.

With this acknowledgment, Job steps back from the role he had slipped into—an unwitting critic of divine governance—and embraces the posture of a creature who trusts the Creator.

Repentance of presumption, not admission of secret sin (42:3–4)

Job quotes God's earlier question: "Who is this that hides counsel without knowledge?" When God first spoke those words, they challenged Job's assumptions. Now Job adopts them as his own confession. He recognizes that he spoke of things beyond his understanding—things "too wonderful" for him, truths too vast to grasp.

It is crucial to see what Job is *not* repenting of. He is not repenting because he caused his own suffering. The prologue and God's own testimony make it clear: Job's suffering was not punishment. Job is not repenting of hidden sin, wickedness, or rebellion. Instead, Job is repenting of the presumption that he could evaluate God's governance of the universe based on his limited experience.

His earlier speeches had drifted into dangerous territory—not blasphemy, but confidence in his own perspective. In demanding that God explain himself, Job implied that he had enough wisdom to judge divine justice. After hearing God's voice, Job sees that he never had the vantage point required to make such evaluations. His repentance is not moral guilt—it is intellectual and spiritual humility.

This repentance is the turning point of the book. Job lays down the burden of trying to run the universe from the ash heap. He yields to a wisdom far greater than his own.

"My ears had heard…but now my eyes have seen" (42:5)

Job's famous statement captures the heart of his transformation. He had always believed in God, always feared him, always honored him. But now the God he trusted has stepped into his suffering in a way Job could never have anticipated.

Job does not mean he has literally seen God's face—that would contradict other Scripture. Rather, he has encountered God's presence and character in a deeper, more immediate way. The distance that once existed between Job's theology and Job's experience has collapsed.

Before, Job's understanding of God relied on tradition, observation, and inherited wisdom. Those were not wrong, but they were incomplete. Suffering had shaken Job's categories, and God's revelation rebuilt them with a grandeur and humility Job had never known.

Seeing God does not answer Job's questions, but it makes the questions smaller. The world is still mysterious, but the One who governs it has revealed himself. Job has moved from hearsay to encounter, from analysis to worship.

Repentance as humility, not guilt (42:6)

Job concludes: "Therefore I despise myself and repent in dust and ashes." This verse is often misunderstood. Job is not saying he hates himself or that he is worthless. The phrase "I despise myself" can mean "I retract my case" or "I withdraw my complaint." Job is abandoning his court summons, his lawsuit against God, his insistence that he deserved an explanation.

Job's repentance is the expression of a righteous man humbled by divine glory. It is the step of someone who realizes that his earlier words, while spoken in pain, went beyond his limits. Job repents not of immorality but of his assumption that he could understand God's ways if only God would explain them.

This humility is not humiliation—it is healing. Dust and ashes were the posture of grief; now they become the posture of surrender. Job's repentance is the beginning of restoration. Before God restores anything material, he restores Job's heart to a place of awe-filled trust.

Righteousness and humility can coexist in a sufferer

Job's repentance demonstrates that righteousness does not equal perfection and humility does not equal guilt. Job's integrity remains intact—God will soon vindicate him publicly in verse 7. But even righteous sufferers must guard against the subtle pride that comes when pain tempts us to believe we see the world clearly.

Job's repentance shows that humility is not confession of wrongdoing but recognition of creaturely limits. Job bows not because he sinned, but because he has seen God.

And this is the great irony of the book: the man who once longed for a trial now abandons his case, not because he lost, but because he finally understands that the Judge is far greater than the trial.

Encounter, not explanation, brings transformation

God still has not explained the heavenly council, the accuser, or the purpose of Job's suffering. God has not justified himself. God has not revealed any hidden sin in Job. Instead, God has revealed himself.

And that is enough.

Job's heart, wounded and bewildered, finds rest not in information but in revelation. The righteous sufferer does not need all the answers—he needs the presence of the God who commands the morning and governs the depths. Job's repentance is not a retreat from faith but a deeper entrance into it.

This is the shift that prepares Job for restoration. His questions are quieter now, not because suffering is explained but because God has been seen. The encounter changes everything.

APPLICATION

1. Repentance can mean releasing presumption, not confessing wrongdoing

Job shows that repentance is not always about guilt—sometimes it is about letting go of assumptions we were never meant to carry. In suffering, Christians often slip into the belief that if God would only explain himself, everything would make sense. We begin to act as though our perspective is the standard by which God should operate. Job's repentance is the recognition that he had taken on a role too heavy for a creature. Christians today face the same temptation. Pain narrows our world, and we begin to speak boldly about what God *should* do or how he *must* act. Job teaches that part of faithfulness is repenting of the presumption that we can judge God's governance. Letting go of that illusion is not weakness—it is the beginning of peace.

2. Seeing God clearly changes how we see everything else

Job's transformation happens when he moves from hearing about God to encountering God. Nothing in Job's circumstances has changed—his wounds remain, his losses remain, and his questions remain. But his vision of God has changed, and therefore his heart can rest. Believers today sometimes wait for life to improve before they feel they can trust again. But Scripture shows that trust grows not from improved circumstances but from renewed understanding of who God is. When we behold God's character—his power, holiness, compassion, and wisdom—our suffering no longer feels like evidence against him. Job's renewed vision reminds Christians that intimacy with God steadies the soul more than answers ever could. Seeing God clearly brings courage to endure what we cannot understand.

3. Humility guards even the righteous from dangerous assumptions

Job's repentance shows that humility is not only for the guilty; it is essential even for the righteous. Job was upright, blameless, and deeply devoted. Yet his suffering tempted him to assume he could evaluate God's justice from the ash heap. This is a danger believers still face. When life hurts, we begin to believe that our perspective is complete, our conclusions are accurate, and our judgments are justified. But humility reminds us that we are limited creatures. It protects us from believing that God must fit within our understanding. Job's example encourages Christians to practice humility not as self-condemnation but as wisdom—recognizing that God's ways are higher, deeper, and wiser than our own. Humility keeps the heart soft and the faith steady.

4. Encountering God leads to surrender, and surrender leads to rest

Job's final act before restoration is not a theological argument but a humble surrender: "I retract my case and repent in dust and ashes." This surrender is not despair—it is relief. Job no longer needs to carry the burden of explaining or defending or understanding. He entrusts himself to the God he now sees more clearly. Christians often try to force rest by solving their problems, mastering their questions, or controlling their circumstances. But Scripture teaches that rest flows from surrender. When believers release the need for answers and embrace the God who holds all things together, their hearts find peace even before their circumstances change. Job shows that surrender is not the end of faith—it is the doorway into deeper trust and renewed hope.

CONCLUSION

Job 42:1–6 marks the moment when Job's heart finally comes to rest. God has not answered Job's questions, exposed hidden sin, or explained the purpose of his suffering. Instead, God has revealed his greatness, and that revelation changes everything. Job's repentance is not an admission of guilt but a surrender of the belief that he could evaluate God's justice from his limited vantage point. Seeing God clearly—after so many chapters of hearsay, debate, and anguish—reshapes his entire understanding of what it means to trust.

Job lets go of the courtroom, the arguments, and the demand for explanations. He takes his place as a humble worshiper before a wise Creator. And this is the hinge on which the entire book turns. Restoration will come, but it will come to a man whose heart has been reoriented by awe. Before anything in Job's life is healed, his vision is restored. That is the true beginning of renewal.

REFLECTION

1. How does Job's shift from demanding explanations to beholding God speak into your own struggles?

2. Where might you need to repent not of wrongdoing, but of assuming you see the whole picture?

3. How does Job's confession, "now my eyes have seen you," challenge the way you approach God in suffering?

4. What limits of your own understanding has God exposed in difficult seasons?

5. Why is humility such an important posture for believers who desire deeper trust in God?

6. Where do you sense God inviting you to lay down the burden of having to understand everything?

DISCUSSION

1. Why is it significant that Job's repentance centers on presumption rather than moral guilt?

2. How does Job 42:1–6 demonstrate that righteous people can still need humility?

3. What does Job mean when he says he had only "heard" of God before but now has "seen" him?

4. How does God's revelation—not explanation—change Job's entire perspective on suffering?

5. What dangers arise when believers assume their perspective is sufficient to judge God's ways?

6. How can the church help Christians cultivate humility and trust during seasons of confusion or pain?

12

JOB'S RESTORATION

JOB 42:7-17

Objective: To understand how God vindicates Job, corrects the friends, and restores Job through grace rather than explanation.

INTRODUCTION

In 1967, seventeen-year-old Joni Eareckson dove into the Chesapeake Bay, misjudged the depth, and broke her neck. In an instant, she went from an athletic, active teenager to a quadriplegic. The months that followed were filled with brutal questions: Why did God allow this? Had she done something to deserve it? Friends and visitors tried to help, but some offered shallow explanations that only deepened the pain. Joni writes about staring at the ceiling of a hospital room, wondering if she could ever trust God again when her life had been so completely upended.

Over time, she did not receive a neat explanation from heaven. Instead, she encountered the God who met her in suffering, reshaped her character, and used her story to strengthen countless Christians around the world. Her life became a living testimony that faith can grow even when answers do not come.

Job 42:7-17 carries us into a similar space. After long chapters of accusation and confusion, God finally speaks—not to explain everything, but to vindicate Job's trust and correct the friends' theology. Restoration begins as God reorders relationships, calls for intercession, and quietly rebuilds a broken life. This passage helps us see that God's concern is not simply to end our pain, but to reveal his character, heal his people, and teach us to trust him when the reasons remain hidden.

EXAMINATION

God's verdict on Job and his friends (42:7)

When God turns from Job to address the friends, the tone of the book shifts dramatically. For the first time since the prologue, God speaks *about* Job rather than *to* him. What he says is both surprising and decisive. God tells Eliphaz, "My anger burns against you and your two friends, for you have not spoken of me what is right, as my servant Job has." It is a moment of public vindication. Throughout the book, the friends believed they were defending God. They interpreted Job's suffering through a rigid framework in which the righteous prosper and the wicked suffer. Though their intentions may have been sincere, their theology reduced God to a predictable system rather than a sovereign, wise Creator whose purposes transcend human logic.

God's rebuke exposes their error: they had spoken confidently about matters far beyond their understanding. Job, despite his anguish and bold complaints, remained a man of integrity. His questions came from honesty and grief, not arrogance. He had wrestled openly with God rather than hiding behind tidy formulas. God affirms that Job's struggle—even with all its raw emotion—was closer to truth than the friends' rigid certainty. In this moment, the book's central tension is resolved not by justifying Job's suffering, but by clarifying whose voice represented God faithfully.

The friends' dependence on Job's intercession (42:8–9)

God not only rebukes the friends—he instructs them to bring sacrifices and seek Job's prayers. This is one of the most profound reversals in the entire story. The men who accused Job of hypocrisy must now ask Job, the man they dismissed, to stand between them and divine wrath. Job's role in the prologue quietly reappears. He began the story offering sacrifices for his children; he now offers prayer for his friends. The symmetry is intentional. Before Job's fortunes are restored, his priestly calling is restored.

This act of intercession is not symbolic; it is relational. God restores Job to fellowship with his community by making him the means through which others find forgiveness. It is also a quiet testimony to Job's healed heart. The man who suffered under their accusations now prays for their forgiveness without bitterness. Job's integrity is not merely declared by God; it is embodied in his actions.

Restoration begins in relationships, not in wealth (42:10–11)

When Scripture says "the Lord restored the fortunes of Job," the reader may expect a return to prosperity. Yet the first sign of renewal is not financial—it is relational. Job's brothers, sisters, and former acquaintances return to him. They share a meal in his home, an act that reflects reconciliation, trust, and restored fellowship. They mourn with him and comfort him for all the disaster the Lord had allowed. Their presence cannot undo his grief, but their return signals a shift from isolation to community—a vital step in the healing process.

Job's suffering had driven people away, not necessarily out of cruelty but discomfort. Now restoration begins with people returning, offering sympathy, and sharing their resources with him. Before God doubles Job's possessions, he restores what suffering had fractured: the human connections that sustain a faithful life. Healing almost always begins with presence before prosperity.

A restoration shaped by grace, not formula (42:10, 12–15)

The doubling of Job's flock and herds is striking, but the narrator never presents it as payment for righteousness. Job's restoration is an act of grace, not wages earned. If blessing were simply a reward for worthy behavior, then the friends' theology would be validated. But the Lord restores Job after condemning their simplistic retribution model. What Job receives is not compensation but generosity—gift rather than guarantee.

The mention of Job's new family deepens that truth. He receives seven sons and three daughters, echoing the earlier structure of his home but not replacing the children he lost. Scripture does not suggest the new children erase the memory or pain of the first ten; rather, they represent God's kindness in rebuilding a life devastated by sorrow. The daughters receive special mention, including the fact that Job gives them an inheritance alongside their brothers—an extraordinary gesture in the ancient world. This detail portrays Job's renewed vitality, compassion, and generosity. His prosperity is now marked not only by abundance but by grace.

God's governance is upheld, even when unexplained (42:12–17)

By the end of the book, one reality becomes clear: God does not reveal the heavenly council scene to Job. The wager, the accuser, the reasons for Job's suffering—all remain hidden. Job never learns why he suffered, but he learns who governs the world. That knowledge is enough. God's ways do not need defending; they need beholding. The purpose of the book is not to solve the problem of suffering but to correct narrow expectations about how God must act.

The friends believed justice was always immediate. Job believed justice required explanation. God reveals a universe that operates with wisdom more expansive than either viewpoint allowed. Job's renewed blessing does not prove the friends' theology; it proves God's freedom. He gives and withholds according to his wisdom, not human formulas.

A closing marked by blessing, not naivety (42:16–17)

The story ends quietly: Job lives 140 more years, sees four generations, and dies "full of days." The phrase echoes patriarchal blessing, signaling a life marked by grace and fullness. It does not imply that Job never grieved again or that restoration erased the shadows of loss. Instead, it affirms that God met Job in his suffering, sustained him through it, and brought him into a season of renewed meaning. Restoration in Scripture rarely erases the past; it reorients the future.

Job's story ends not with answers but with God's presence, with faith renewed, and with life rebuilt through grace. The final image we are given is not Job as the man on the ash heap but Job as a man whose trust has deepened, whose humility has matured, and whose relationship with God has been restored to joy. The God who allowed Job's suffering now surrounds his servant with blessing, dignity, and peace.

APPLICATION

1. Trusting God means releasing the urge to explain suffering

The book closes by showing that Job never receives the explanation he once demanded, yet he finds peace because he releases the need to unravel the mysteries of providence. This is a crucial lesson for believers. When we suffer, our hearts instinctively search for reasons—something to hold, something to make sense of our pain. But God's response to Job teaches that explanations are not the foundation of faith. Trust grows when we surrender the assumption that we can judge God's purposes from our limited perspective. Job's humility becomes our model: he lets go of his case against God and entrusts himself to the One whose wisdom exceeds human understanding. Christians today find rest not in decoding suffering, but in submitting to the God who stands above it.

2. Speaking rightly about God requires humility and restraint

The friends' mistake was not devotion but confidence without humility. They believed they understood how God must govern the world. In their certainty, they misrepresented God and wounded Job. God's rebuke reminds believers that humility is not optional in theology—it is essential. When Christians speak about suffering, providence, or justice, we must do so with caution, remembering our limitations. Job's honest struggle was closer to truth than the friends' confident answers because he refused to pretend he understood what he could not. Faithful speech about God begins with reverence, continues with caution, and ends with surrender. Christians must resist the temptation to fill silence with assumptions, choosing instead to speak with gentleness and humility.

3. Restoration is an act of grace, not a formula to predict

Job's renewed blessings are gifts from God, not wages earned. That distinction matters. If Job's restoration were payment for his righteousness, the friends' theology would be correct—good things happen to good people, bad things happen to bad people, and the world runs like a moral vending machine. But God restores Job only after dismantling that simplistic view. His generosity is rooted in compassion and wisdom, not in obligation. This teaches believers to view blessings with gratitude rather than entitlement. God's kindness is real, but it is not mechanical. Christians can rejoice in seasons of restoration without assuming they "deserved" it, and they can endure seasons of suffering without assuming they caused it. Grace, not formula, governs the life of faith.

4. Healing often comes through restored relationships

The first evidence of God's renewal in Job's life is not doubled livestock but the return of family and friends. They come to comfort him, to eat with him, and to rebuild community around him. This reveals a profound truth: healing is often relational. God designed his people to be strengthened through presence, compassion, and shared life. When believers walk through suffering, they need more than theological answers—they need people who will sit in their grief and stand beside them as life is rebuilt. Job's restored community reflects the church's calling to embody God's presence through fellowship, encouragement, and shared burdens. When Christians draw near to the hurting, they participate in God's work of restoration.

CONCLUSION

Job's story ends not with answers, but with God's presence and favor. The Lord publicly affirms Job's integrity, rebukes the friends' narrow theology, and restores Job's role as intercessor—a role marked by humility, compassion, and renewed fellowship. Restoration comes, but it comes as grace, not as payment or reward. Job's suffering was never a sign of divine rejection, and his blessing is never presented as divine repayment.

The final picture we see is a man whose faith has been deepened rather than destroyed. His community returns. His family grows. His life extends into old age, marked by meaning and fullness. But even these blessings do not undo the reality of his grief; instead, they testify that God's goodness can fill a life that has known great sorrow. Job's tale closes with quiet dignity—an invitation to trust the God whose wisdom governs both suffering and restoration, and whose grace is sufficient even when explanations are withheld.

REFLECTION

1. How does God's vindication of Job reshape your understanding of faithful lament?

2. Where might you be tempted—like the friends—to speak confidently about things you do not fully understand?

3. Why is it important to recognize that Job's restoration comes as grace rather than repayment?

4. How do restored relationships in this chapter challenge you to value community in seasons of suffering?

5. Where do you sense God calling you to release your need for explanations and trust his wisdom instead?

6. How does Job's willingness to intercede for those who hurt him shape your understanding of forgiveness?

DISCUSSION

1. What does God's rebuke of the friends teach us about the dangers of rigid theological systems?

2. How does Job's role as an intercessor reflect God's approval of him and restore his spiritual leadership?

3. Why is it significant that restoration begins with community before material blessing?

4. How does this chapter challenge the idea that prosperity is always a sign of God's favor?

5. Why do you think God never explains the heavenly council scene or the cause of Job's suffering to him?

6. How can the church reflect Job's restored community by supporting those who suffer today?

13

THE MESSAGE OF JOB

Objective: To grasp the book of Job's message about suffering, wisdom, humility, and the God who speaks in sovereign grace.

INTRODUCTION

In 2010, researchers completed a decades-long project known as the Human Genome Project, mapping all three billion base pairs of human DNA. One scientist involved in the project reflected on the experience by saying, "The closer we looked, the more complexity we found. Every answer opened ten new questions. But what we gained wasn't control—it was wonder."

The more they learned, the more they realized how much remained beyond their grasp. Their expanding knowledge did not shrink the mystery; it deepened their reverence for the intricacy of life.

The book of Job produces a similar effect. It does not simplify the mysteries of suffering. It does not offer tidy answers or reduce God's ways to formulas. Instead, Job expands our vision. It forces believers to see that the universe is larger, God's wisdom deeper, and human understanding more limited than we often admit. Through Job's lament, the friends' errors, God's overwhelming speeches, and Job's humble repentance, we learn that the life of faith is not built on mastering explanations but on trusting the God whose greatness exceeds our questions.

As the book concludes, Job is not given a key to unlock all of life's puzzles. He is given something better—the presence, favor, and restoration of the God who has been with him all along. Job's story invites every Christian to trade certainty for humility, analysis for worship, and demand for trust. This is the path to wisdom.

EXAMINATION

The book of Job closes with blessing, but it does not begin there, and it certainly does not travel there quickly. To grasp its message, readers must hold the entire journey together—the quiet righteousness of Job's early life, the violent collapse of everything he treasured, the long wrestling in ashes, the bewildering counsel of friends, the piercing questions of the whirlwind, the humble repentance of a righteous sufferer, and the gracious restoration given by God. Job is not a book that yields simple lessons. It is a book that reshapes the way believers understand suffering, wisdom, and the God who governs the world with justice deeper than our explanations.

At the heart of Job is the reality that the righteous may suffer without any wrongdoing. The opening chapters leave no ambiguity: Job is upright, blameless, and God's own commendation of him echoes through the heavenly council. His suffering is not retribution; it is mystery. The friends cannot conceive of innocent suffering. Their understanding of God leaves no room for unpredictability, and so they force Job into a narrative he does not fit. Job becomes a test case for their assumptions rather than a brother to be comforted.

Job's story teaches that wisdom begins with acknowledging this truth: the world is not a tidy place where blessing always signals righteousness and hardship always signals sin. The friends' error is not that they value justice but that they assume they understand its timing and mechanics. They defend God as though he needs their protection and speak confidently about divine justice without considering the limits of human perspective. Their theology is too small for the world God made.

Yet Job also shows that righteous suffering, though it is real, must still be carried humbly. Job's grief is understandable. His lament is honest, raw, and unfiltered. Scripture never rebukes him for expressing his anguish. In fact, God later affirms that Job has spoken of him truly. But even a righteous sufferer can drift into presumption when pain narrows vision. Job reaches moments where he longs not simply for relief but for an explanation, a chance to challenge God's fairness. He wants the universe to make sense under his scrutiny. Pain tempts even the faithful to think their limited view is complete.

This tension sets the stage for God's entrance. When the Lord finally speaks, he does not solve Job's questions; he enlarges Job's world. The divine speeches from the whirlwind do not explain suffering—they reveal the God who governs creation with power, wisdom, and intimate care. God directs Job's attention to the foundations of the earth, the rhythms of dawn and darkness, and the storehouses of weather beyond human reach. He shows Job the wildness of creation: lions, mountain goats, ravens, wild donkeys, untamable oxen, the war horse that revels in battle, the hawk that takes flight by instinct, and the eagle that builds its nest on high. These creatures live beyond human oversight yet squarely within God's.

God's intent is not to overwhelm Job with displays of power but to show him something deeper: the world is far more intricate, expansive, and wondrous than any human mind can grasp. Job has tried to evaluate God's justice using the narrow window of his own suffering; God shows him a universe filled with mysteries too great for quick explanations. The friends believed they understood God by observing life's patterns. Job believed he could understand God if given enough reasons. God reveals that neither approach reaches the truth. Wisdom begins with reverent humility before the Creator whose knowledge is unsearchable.

The climax of this revelation comes with Behemoth and Leviathan. These creatures—massive, mysterious, described in poetic grandeur—represent forces beyond human mastery. Behemoth is serene strength; Leviathan is untamable terror. Job cannot subdue them, but God delights in their existence. They embody the idea that God's governance includes both order and wildness. The world is not fragile, nor is it chaotic; it is God-ruled in ways that surpass human expectations. Job's suffering felt like Leviathan—a force that rose from the deep, uninvited and overwhelming. Yet God points to Leviathan as a creature under his rule. If God controls what terrifies Job, then Job can trust the God who controls his circumstances.

When Job finally speaks in chapter 42, it becomes clear that the encounter—not explanation—has transformed him. Job does not confess hidden sin. He repents of presumption. He retracts his case against God. He acknowledges that he spoke of things too wonderful for him. His humility is not shame but clarity. His repentance is not confession of guilt but recognition of creaturely limits. Job no longer needs to interrogate divine justice;

he has seen the Judge. "My ears had heard of you," he says, "but now my eyes have seen you." That insight changes everything.

God's next act vindicates Job publicly. In front of the very men who accused him, God declares Job to have spoken rightly. The friends' theology collapses. Their simplistic understanding of suffering is rejected. And in a moment rich with irony, they must seek Job's intercession to be forgiven. This restores Job to the role he held in the book's opening—intercessor, priestly mediator for those he loves. Job prays for the friends who wounded him, and God accepts his prayer.

Only then does restoration begin. But Scripture is careful to show that restoration begins with people, not possessions. Job's family and acquaintances return to him, offering compassion and presence before prosperity. Healing begins with community. When blessing finally comes, it is lavish yet unmistakably framed as grace. Doubling Job's possessions is not repayment for righteousness; it is divine generosity that stands outside any formula. God's blessing does not erase Job's scars, nor does it suggest that every grief is undone. But it shows that suffering is not the final word.

This ending does not flatten Job's story into a moral lesson; it enriches it with hope. God remains sovereign, even when his ways are hidden. Wisdom demands humility, not certainty. Righteous suffering exists, but so does divine faithfulness. Lament can be faithful speech. Honest questions are not threats to God. Restoration does not erase pain, yet it testifies that God can fill a life with meaning after loss. Job's perseverance, celebrated later in Scripture, points forward to the ultimate righteous sufferer—Jesus—who entrusted himself to God even when surrounded by darkness, and whose resurrection became the ultimate act of divine vindication.

The book closes quietly, but its message resounds. Wisdom is not found in mastering life's mysteries but in trusting the One who governs them. Faith does not demand answers; it seeks the God who speaks. And the God who answered Job still answers his people—not always with explanations, but always with presence, mercy, and grace.

APPLICATION

1. Hold suffering with humility rather than certainty

Job's story teaches believers to resist the temptation to explain what we cannot possibly understand. The friends were certain they knew why Job suffered, and that certainty allowed them to wound a righteous man. Their mistake warns Christians today: suffering is not a puzzle we are called to solve but a burden we are called to carry with humility. When we assume God must follow our formulas, we inevitably distort his character and misrepresent his ways. Job shows that faith does not mean decoding every hardship; it means trusting the God who governs the world wisely even when life makes no sense. Humility opens space for compassion, honesty, and reverence—three things the friends lacked and Job recovered only when he saw God clearly.

2. Lament can be faithful, honest, and holy

One of Job's greatest gifts to believers is his courage to bring unfiltered pain into God's presence. His lament is raw, but it is not rebellious. God later affirms Job's honesty and rejects the friends' polished but misguided speeches. This teaches the church that God prefers truthful anguish over polite falsehood. Believers suffering loss, depression, chronic illness, or unanswered questions should feel permission to cry out to God without fear of being rejected. Lament does not weaken faith—it strengthens it by keeping the heart connected to the One who heals. Job's prayers demonstrate that Christian maturity includes the freedom to speak candidly before God, trusting that he welcomes our honesty and meets us in our sorrow.

3. Trust grows through encounter rather than explanation

God did not explain Job's suffering; he revealed himself. That insight is crucial for Christians today who imagine that peace will come once they understand the reasons behind hardship. Job teaches that peace comes from the presence of God, not the clarity of circumstances. When believers encounter God in Scripture, prayer, worship, and the life of the church, their perspective begins to shift. The fog does not always lift, but God becomes visible through it. Trust deepens not because we gain control but because we hand control back to the God who commands the morning and governs the depths. Job's transformation reminds us that seeing God—even when suffering remains—changes the way we endure, interpret, and ultimately survive seasons of pain.

4. God restores with grace, not formulas, and often through community

Job's restoration is not repayment for righteousness; it is an act of divine kindness. God doubles Job's possessions and blesses him with children, but Scripture never suggests he "earned" this. The blessing comes after God has dismantled every simplistic assumption about suffering and reward. Christians should therefore receive blessings with gratitude rather than entitlement. At the same time, Job's renewal begins not with prosperity but with people—family, friends, and community returning to comfort him. Healing often begins with presence, listening, and shared life. The church becomes a place where God's restoring work is expressed through compassion, encouragement, and practical support. Restoration rarely erases old wounds, but it fills life with new meaning, relationships, and hope.

CONCLUSION

The book of Job does not end with a solved equation—it ends with a transformed man. Job began as a righteous sufferer who endured unimaginable loss. He wrestled honestly, prayed boldly, and sometimes spoke beyond his understanding. But through every stage of sorrow, confusion, and longing, God remained near. When the Lord finally revealed himself from the whirlwind, Job discovered that divine presence outweighs divine explanation.

The friends' narrow theology collapsed under the weight of God's majesty, and Job's humility became the gateway to his renewal. Restoration came not as repayment for righteousness but as a gift rooted in God's grace. Job's scars did not vanish, yet his story closed with meaning, fellowship, and hope.

This final chapter invites believers to walk with the same trust. Suffering will come, answers may not, and life will rarely fit our formulas. But the God who commands creation, hears lament, corrects presumption, restores community, and blesses in grace remains faithful. Wisdom begins when we acknowledge our limits and rest in his sovereign care. And like Job, we learn that the One who speaks out of the whirlwind also stays with us in the ashes.

REFLECTION

1. How has the book of Job reshaped the way you think about innocent suffering?

2. Where do you see yourself in Job's struggle—his questions, his honesty, or his need for humility?

3. What part of God's whirlwind speeches most changed your understanding of his wisdom and power?

4. Why is it important to embrace God's presence even when he withholds explanations?

5. How does Job's story encourage you to rest in God's grace rather than in predictable formulas?

6. Where might God be inviting you to walk in deeper trust, even without answers?

DISCUSSION

1. How does Job challenge the idea that suffering always reveals sin or judgment?

2. In what ways do the friends' speeches warn against rigid or overly confident theology?

3. How do God's creation speeches shape our understanding of divine sovereignty?

4. Why is Job's repentance in chapter 42 an example of humility rather than guilt?

5. How does the restoration of Job's community model the church's role in supporting the suffering?

6. What does Job teach us about faith that endures in the absence of explanations?

www.ingramcontent.com/pod-product-compliance
Lightning Source LLC
Chambersburg PA
CBHW070154080526
44586CB00015B/1979